OVER THERE

America in the Great War

Robert J. Dalessandro
and Rebecca S. Dalessandro

Foreword by
Commissioner Libby O'Connell, Ph.D.,
Chief Historian for the History Channel

STACKPOLE
BOOKS

0 11557 01485 3

To America's sons and daughters who never returned from the War to End All Wars, and to those Soldiers, Sailors, Airmen, Marines, and Coast Guardsmen who serve today.

Copyright © 2016 by Stackpole Books

Published by
STACKPOLE BOOKS
5067 Ritter Road
Mechanicsburg, PA 17055
www.stackpolebooks.com

Printed in the United States of America

10 9 8 7 6 5 4 3 2 1

Cover design by Caroline M. Stover
Front cover photo courtesy of MCHC
Back cover photos courtesy of NARA

Library of Congress Cataloging-in-Publication Data TK

Dalessandro, Robert J., author.
  Over there : America in the Great War / Robert J. Dalessandro and
Rebecca S. Dalessandro ; foreword by Commissioner Libby O'Connell, Ph.D.,
Chief Historian for the History Channel.
     pages cm. — (Stackpole military photo series)
  ISBN 978-0-8117-1485-3
1. World War, 1914-1918—United States—Pictorial works. I. Dalessandro,
Rebecca S., author. II. Title.
  D570.D26 2016
  940.4'0973—dc23
                                  2015027332

CONTENTS

"At present, I am a poet trying to be a soldier. To tell the truth, I am not interested in writing nowadays, except in so far as writing is the expression of something beautiful. . . . The only sort of book I care to write about the war is the sort people will read after the war is over—a century after it is over."

—Sgt. Joyce Kilmer, 165th Infantry Regiment,
42nd Division, killed in action, Seringes-et-Nesles,
France, July 30, 1918

FOREWORD

Photographs not only tell a thousand words, but also capture drama and pathos in a way that words never can. Robert Capa's handful of out-of-focus photographs from a Normandy beach capture the urgency of the D-Day landing better, or at least differently, than written narratives, while Alexander Gardner's photographs after the battle of Antietam uniquely convey the destruction and stillness of death. A photographic record is therefore essential to the comprehension of war.

This compilation of photos showing America's involvement in World War I is especially important because it depicts a war that is central to American and world history but is too little remembered by Americans. For a variety of reasons, World War I has a much fainter imprint on the American consciousness than our two other great wars: the Civil War and World War II. We have a sharply defined sense of the Civil War, not just because of its place in our national history and our ability to walk its battlefields, but also because of the wealth of photographs and illustrations generated by a war waged in our homeland. We have a vivid mind's eye of World War II, not just because of its moral clarity and the national triumph it represents, but also because the war was so vividly documented in radio, newsreels, and newspaper and magazine photographs. Both wars have been frequently and richly—and recently—depicted in popular film, from *Gone With The Wind* to *Glory* and *Cold Mountain*, from *The Big Red One* to *Saving Private Ryan* and *Band of Brothers*.

Not so World War I. It is distant in time, it was fought overseas, news coverage was less immediate, ambivalence surrounded the reasons for the war and its denouement, and U.S. forces fought for a relatively brief period of time. But in that short period, Americans fought with the same tenacity they did in World War II, and they died at a rate surpassed only in the Civil War. Hence the importance of this volume, which aims to bring to life and honor the service of more than 4 million American men and women in a war that, for many, exists only in a handful of posed photographs and grainy snippets of film footage.

This book is published in the midst of the centennial of the Great War, one year before the 100-year anniversary of America's entry into that war. The U.S. World War I Centennial Commission—chartered by the Congress and given the mission of educating the American people about World War I, commemorating the American role in the war, and honoring the courage and sacrifice of American servicemen and women in the war—is proud that its chairman, Robert Dalessandro, along with his wife, Rebecca, have authored this compilation, which will do so much to inform and inspire Americans of all generations.

Commissioner Libby O'Connell, Ph.D.,
Chief Historian for the History Channel

FRANCE

National Highway
Battle Line March 20, 1918
International Boundary

0 25 50 75 100 MILES
0 50 100 KILOMETERS

INTRODUCTION

We live in the long shadow of World War I. One hundred years later, this war is largely overlooked in the United States, eclipsed by the cataclysm that followed during World War II and America's more substantial contribution to the effort necessary to defeat the Axis Powers.

Ironically, it would be the first world war of the fledgling twentieth century and not the second that would thrust a reluctant America unwillingly onto the world stage. The war would open a new American century and spawn the "Greatest Generation." Its legacy would shape the world throughout the decades and conflicts that followed.

The acts of terror that have become such a predictable part of life in the twenty-first century are rooted directly in the outcome of World War I. This war was shaped by a collision of political, economic, and social forces—it precipitated the final collapse of the great monarchies of Europe, it facilitated the rise of Communism, it introduced the world to the concept of self-determination of people, and it created the modern Middle East. The victors of the war, focused on punishment of the vanquished and the restoration of the status quo, ignorantly shaped a postwar world ready-made for the resumption of hostilities. Unaware of the complexities and interplay of Islam, Judaism, and the Middle East in general, the oblivious views and decisions of policymakers in England and France tied the Gordian knot that is the Middle East of our time.

As with any anniversary period, the centennial is important because it gives us an opportunity to reflect on the history of an event. Simply stated, the study of our past, and particularly the importance of an understanding of the catastrophic events of the First World War, strengthens the resolve of our actions and informs our future.

Today's geopolitical environment resembles the state of the world that preceded this tragic war. As such, it is imperative that we understand World War I today, so we do not repeat the decisions and policies that led to that terrible war.

THE WAR BEGINS

When Europe erupted in war during the summer of 1914, Americans reacted with caution. The conflict had broken out in another hemisphere, and initially it appeared that the United States need not become directly involved. Democratic president Woodrow Wilson, who was reelected in 1916, campaigned on the slogan, "He kept us out of war," and many Americans rejoiced that this war was an ocean away. Those Americans following the conflict generally sympathized with England and France, members of the Triple Entente with Russia, and saw Germany and its ally, Austria-Hungary, as the aggressors, particularly after the German invasion of Belgium. However, most Americans considered the war to be Europe's problem, not theirs. Indeed, substantial minorities of Americans were anti-British, anti-Russian, or pro-German.

As the war progressed, American popular opinion increasingly swung in favor of the Allies. By fall 1914, the prospect of a long, drawn-out conflict led the British navy to blockade the North Sea and deny trade from entering German ports. Unable to secure the use of the sea lanes for itself, Germany responded by using its submarines, or U-boats, to attack Allied and neutral merchant ships in an attempt to cut off the United Kingdom from supplies and military aid.

On March 28, 1915, the British steamship RMS *Falaba* was torpedoed and sunk by a German U-boat. Over 100 souls perished, including an American passenger, Leon Chester Thrasher. The event was followed by a flurry of media criticism demanding action against Germany. Anger from the "Thrasher Incident" had barely cooled when, on May 7, 1915, a German U-boat torpedo sank the RMS *Lusitania*, which was carrying both civilian passengers and munitions, off the coast of Ireland. The *Lusitania* disaster took the lives of 1,198 of her passengers and crew, including 128 Americans, provoking outrage in the United States. Submarine attacks were particularly disturbing as they came without notice, and submarines had neither means nor incentive to rescue passengers or crew.

A week after the *Lusitania* sinking, President Woodrow Wilson declared that the United States was "too proud to fight" and would not enter the war. Germany dramatically restricted submarine operations to avoid further provoking the Americans, and it appeared America would remain neutral.

THE ZIMMERMANN TELEGRAM

By January 1917, the Western Front had been a stalemate for over two years. Attrition, through the English naval blockade of the North Sea and the prolonged bloodshed of trench warfare, was gradually wearing down Germany's military strength. German military leaders believed that the best way to break the impasse was to resume unrestricted submarine warfare on merchant shipping to the United Kingdom. This could devastate the British, who were dependent on imported food—much of it from the United States. Germany recognized that unrestricted submarine warfare would probably draw the United States into the conflict, but believed that enough ships could be sunk to force the United Kingdom to sue for peace before the Americans could effectively intervene. Germany formally resumed unrestricted submarine warfare in February 1917.

This change in German military policy coincided with a significant diplomatic misstep. Arthur Zimmermann, German foreign minister, was directed to draft a secret communiqué to the German Imperial envoy in Mexico. The one-page note outlined a bold and dangerous plan in which Zimmermann instructed the diplomatic mission in Mexico to approach the Mexican government with a proposal that would create an alliance between Germany, Mexico, and Japan. This proposed alliance would bring Mexico and Japan into the war to attack the United States in the event America entered the war on the Allied side as a result of the German submarine policy. The Mexican government was offered assistance and the promise of regaining the territories of Texas, Arizona, and New Mexico lost to them in the nineteenth century.

Due to the total blockade imposed by the Allies on Germany, electronic communication via the telegraph between Germany and the outside world followed a tortuous path. Upon the outbreak of war in 1914, the

British immediately severed Germany's transatlantic cable. This forced the Germans to route all international telegraphy through either neutral countries or cables controlled by the Allies. On January 17, 1917, the communiqué, or "Zimmermann Note," as it would soon be referred to in the Western press, was sent via two cable routes. The first route transmitted the coded message over Swedish cables to the German ambassador in Buenos Aires to forward to the German embassy in Washington, D.C., which would then forward it to the German embassy in Mexico.

The second route boldly used the American embassy in Berlin to deliver the message to the State Department in Washington, which in turn would pass it to the German embassy. That message passed over Dutch cables via London to the United States. President Wilson's avowed neutral administration promised to deliver German diplomatic messages to the world via this method in order to facilitate peace negotiations. This placed the Wilson administration in the embarrassing position of hand-delivering a threat against the United States.

As the note was sent via these two routes, it was intercepted by a secret team of the British intelligence service known as Room 40. The name was derived from the number of the room the team occupied in the old British Admiralty Building. Unknown to anyone outside of this organization, Room 40 had tapped the cable routes and could "read" German telegraph traffic. The message was in a code, or cypher, which used number groups in substitution for words. The Room 40 team recognized the sequence as German code 0075, which the British team had already been "breaking," or translating. Adm. William Hall, director of British Naval Intelligence, kept the knowledge of this intercepted note secret within Room 40 until the full note was translated and its intention understood.

UNRESTRICTED SUBMARINE WARFARE RESUMES

On February 3, 1917, the German government announced the resumption of a policy of unrestricted submarine warfare on commercial shipping heading to Europe. In protest, the United States promptly severed diplomatic ties with Germany, and the U.S. embassy staff left the country on February 10, passing into Switzerland and then France. On February 5, Admiral Hall notified the British Foreign Office of the Zimmermann telegram's contents. The note was recognized as having enormous value to the British strategic goal of turning American public opinion against Germany. But how to leak the note's existence without disclosing the role of Room 40 and the fact that British intelligence was actively reading both German and American diplomatic traffic posed a great problem for the British government. In the month of February alone, German submarine activity had sunk 106 British-flagged merchant vessels, up from 49 the previous month; the situation had become desperate. The submarine campaign would force the British to reveal the telegram's damaging contents to the government of the United States, in the hope that it would reach the American people in time to change the course of the war.

AMERICA DECLARES WAR

Admiral Hall developed a plan of intrigue that would present the American authorities with the contents of the telegram and preserve the secret of the work conducted by Room 40. Hall obtained a copy of the coded message from the Mexico City telegraph office. This would provide the cover story on how the information was obtained, and the code used to transmit the note from the German embassy in Washington to Mexico City was an older German code, number 13040, which had already been broken. On February 22, the contents of the Zimmermann telegram were disclosed to Walter Page, American ambassador to Great Britain. Page was outraged by the note and accepted the story that it was obtained via the Mexican telegraph office. He was asked not to reveal the British government as the source.

Two days later, on February 24, Ambassador Page telegraphed the contents of the Zimmermann note to President Wilson. On February 27, the message was given to the *Associated Press* and hit the American newspapers.

The effect of the telegram was electric, inflaming American popular opinion. This, coupled with the sinking of three American merchant ships by German submarines on March 15, led President Wilson to act. On April 2, 1917, he came before Congress with a request to declare war on Germany. The request had the support of a majority of the country. Four days later, the United States entered World War I on the side of the Allies. For Germany, it was now a race to a position of advantage before the American army could arrive.

AMERICA MOBILIZES

The United States was utterly unprepared for war. At the time, the major combatants were fielding armies comprised of millions of soldiers; the U.S. Army numbered fewer than 130,000. While the U.S. Navy could deploy a modern fleet relatively rapidly, it was ill-equipped for antisubmarine warfare. To raise a national army, Congress passed the Selective Service Act in May 1917, which instituted a system for conscripting men into military service.

During the summer of 1917, a small force of soldiers was sent to Europe. Training camps throughout the United States were rapidly filling with volunteers and draftees. By the fall, divisions of newly trained soldiers began leaving the camps, headed for ships to transport them across the Atlantic. As winter turned into spring, ever-increasing numbers of newly trained soldiers were heading "over there." By July 1918, more than 10,000 U.S. troops were arriving in Europe every day.

American soldiers in the trenches, France, 1918. LOC

CHAPTER 1
DOUGHBOYS, GOBS, AND DEVIL DOGS

GEN. JOHN J. PERSHING ARRIVES

American general John J. Pershing and his staff, constituting the advance party of what would become known as the American Expeditionary Force (AEF), would face an evolving mix of German storm troop doctrine, technological advances, and political-military crisis (including the repercussions of the Russian Revolution), when they landed in Boulogne, France, on June 13, 1917. With the French government fearing the specter of army mutinies akin to those in May 1917, when several demoralized French divisions refused to attack, Pershing's arrival in Paris was carefully orchestrated to allow for the greatest number of people to be out on the streets—just after the shops had closed. The scene was one of pandemonium and national relief.

While Pershing was cheered, great debate raged concerning the type of contribution the United States would make, now that they had declared war. The debate was not unfounded, as the United States possessed a very small standing and reserve army when it entered the world conflict in April 1917, consisting of only 127,588 officers and men serving in the Regular Army, backed by another 80,446 National Guard troops, with a full strength of just 208,000 men. Many of the regulars were serving in units in the Philippine Islands or deployed with portions of the National Guard along the U.S.–Mexican border. When compared to the size of the armies fighting in Europe in 1917, this was a tiny force, hardly worthy of notice by European standards.

Anticipating the need for more men, Congress had passed a draft bill that became law on May 18, 1917. Now, Pershing cabled Washington that a million-man army would need to be raised and sent to France within a year, and that the target size would eventually need to be expanded to 3 million.

America had men to draft, but lacked the specialized weapons and equipment now considered basic necessities on the Western Front to arm them, except for the infantry rifle, a few machine guns of mixed type, and a selection of field artillery. Even though American industry was manufacturing munitions for the Allies, machine guns, tanks, hand grenades, trench mortars, gas masks and chemical weapons, helmets, and adequate heavy trench boots were all nonexistent

in the U.S. Army in April 1917. A handful of planes and trucks had been used on the Mexican border, but the Army did not possess a comprehensive motorized logistical force or air arm.

A critical two months had been lost as the Wilson Administration vacillated as to the type and size of the American commitment. Would the United States send only money and war materiel, just men as filler for Allied units, or attempt to establish a complete American army?

To keep his desire for a distinct American army viable, Pershing would be thrust into the world of diplomacy and coalition building. The British proposed to train and equip 500,000 American men and absorb them into the British Expeditionary Force (BEF) units on the Western Front. The French proposed to equip and integrate American regiments into French divisions along their entire line. None of these schemes were acceptable to Pershing or the leadership of the United States. Army leadership had not been idle since the war erupted in 1914; it had studied the problem of modern organization and developed a plan of infantry divisions, which Congress approved in 1916. Due to a variety of logistical, administrative, and tactical concerns, the size of the American infantry divisions sent to France was actually twice the manpower strength of standard European divisions of both sides, averaging around 28,000 men. (BEF division strength was 15,000 men; French and German divisions averaged 12,000 men each.)

THE UNITED STATES NAVY

After large amounts of low-interest loans were made to the Allies, the first military contribution would come not from the army, but from the navy. As soon as war was declared, the 191 vessels of the United States Navy, 14 of which were of the modern Dreadnought class, actively joined the war effort. The United States Coast Guard was placed under the direction of the U.S. Navy, and many U.S.-flagged merchant vessels were armed with guns and detachments to crew them. Even large motor yachts were pressed into service as picket boats along the coast to watch for submarines. The first operational U.S. combat unit to deploy to France arrived on June 5, 1917, in the form of the 1st Aeronautic

1

Detachment and went into training with French aircraft at the Military Aviation School at Tours. They flew their first antisubmarine combat patrol on November 22, 1917. The focus of the U.S. Navy's operations would be on protecting the convoys of troops and supplies and enforcing the blockade around Europe through patrols and mining operations.

The Department of the Navy also contributed its littoral force, the United States Marines, and ordered the 4th and 5th Marine Brigades to move to France. The 4th Marine Brigade, consisting of the 5th and 6th Marine Regiments and the 6th Marine Machine Gun Battalion, was attached to the Army's 2nd Infantry Division; the 5th Marine Brigade was dispersed throughout the Services of Supply in general support of their logistical mission. Finally, the navy also manned several large-caliber railroad guns in France.

While rush orders were being developed for everything from uniforms to ammunition, the U.S. Army moved quickly to send a division to Europe as a show of force.

LAFAYETTE, NOUS VOILA!

Activated on May 27, 1917 as the headquarters, the 1st Expeditionary Division—under the command of Brig. Gen. William L. Sibert and consisting of men of the 16th, 26th, and 28th Infantry Regiments and 6th Field Artillery Regiment—sailed from Hoboken, New Jersey, on June 13 and arrived in France on June 26 to cheering crowds at the port of St. Nazaire.

To boost French morale, elements of the 16th Infantry paraded down the streets of Paris on July 4. Pershing made a short speech to the cheering crowds at the tomb of the French hero of the American Revolution, the Marquis de Lafayette, but it was another speaker from his staff, Capt. Charles E. Stanton, who remembered our Revolutionary War debt to the French people by ending his speech, in French, with a phrase that summarized the spirit of the day: "*Lafayette, nous voila!*"—Lafayette, we are here!

The American Expeditionary Force (AEF) had arrived, but it would be some time before the Allies could rely on the Americans as a fighting force. It would take nearly a year of logistical organization and training to get them ready for action as an independent army in their own combat zone.

Two days after the parade in Paris, the fledgling American organization was redesignated the 1st Division of the United States Army, AEF. The infantry elements of the division were then sent to Gondrecourt to be outfitted and trained in French methods of trench warfare, while the artillery regiments were forwarded on to an artillery training center at Valdahon.

Before the end of the year, elements of the 1st Infantry Division were attached to the French 18th Division; on September 21, 1917, they went into the line with them. At 6:05 A.M. on October 23, Battery C of the 6th Artillery fired the symbolic first American shot of the war. After nearly six months, the Yanks were finally facing the Germans in the trenches around Bathelémont, north of Lunéville. Here, they would learn to man listening posts and go on combat patrols. They also suffered the first army casualties in combat and were the subject of German raids to take prisoners for intelligence purposes. The Germans wanted to prove to their men that the American soldier was ordinary and could be defeated. The hardy Americans would prove otherwise!

Secretary of War Newton D. Baker, although initially opposed to the war, quickly enacted measures to expand the army and presided over its unprecedented growth. Baker personally selected Gen. John J. Pershing to lead the AEF. LOC

President Woodrow Wilson, sits at his desk with his wife, Edith Bolling Galt, standing at his side. After the United States entered the war, Wilson became progressively enchanted with the idea of an international body designed to keep the peace. LOC

A soldier from the New York National Guard saying goodbye to his sweetheart in 1917. NARA

Artist James Montgomery Flagg stands by his iconic poster of World War I, portraying a scowling Uncle Sam declaring, "I want you for the U.S. Army." Although Flagg's poster is most remembered today, it had far less impact on recruiting than other posters released at the time. NARA

On the eve of World War I, the small American army and navy were designed to protect America's borders and her newly acquired overseas possessions. In order to fight a protracted war in Europe, the Armed Forces would need to rapidly expand through both volunteers and a draft. In this photo, the first capsule of the second draft is drawn from a bowl by Secretary of War Baker. NARA

Naval reserves gather in New York City.
NARA

For the first time, significant numbers of women in uniform were intricately involved in a national struggle. In this image, San Francisco, California, Yeomanettes attached to the Naval Reserve, Twelfth District, salute as the national colors pass. NARA

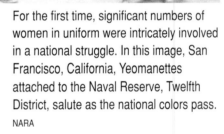

A Newark, New Jersey, mother escorts her son to a train bound for an army training camp. NARA

The original caption for this photo reads: "Are We Downhearted? You don't have to hear their answer to know these men on their way to Camp Upton [New York] are not. These men from New York are radiating their joy at getting into the Nation's service." As with previous wars, most young men were afraid they would miss their chance at the great adventure. NARA

Vocational training for the Student Army Training Corps, a predecessor to the Reserve Officers' Training Corps (ROTC), at the University of Michigan–Ann Arbor. Here, students take a break during a class on pole climbing. Field telegraphs and telephones were still the preferred means of communication during World War I. NARA

The wireless, or radio, was just coming of age. Here, men are taught basic radio work under direction of the Federal Vocational Board. These students practice transmitting messages to classmates at Stuyvesant Evening High School, New York. NARA

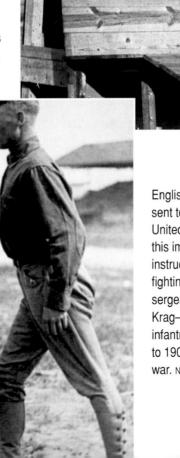

Recruits scaling a wall obstacle at Camp Wadsworth, South Carolina. Obstacle courses became standard fare for new soldiers as the army began preparing them for the rigors of trench warfare. NARA

English and French instructors were sent to training camps throughout the United States to help train soldiers. In this image, a British sergeant major instructs a young recruit on bayonet fighting at Camp Dick, Texas. The sergeant major holds an outmoded Krag–Jørgensen rifle, the primary infantry weapon of the Army from 1894 to 1903, relegated to training during the war. NARA

The navy also radically expanded. Here, members of the navy militia train at Somersville, New York. NARA

A clever doughboy puts his gas mask to good use while peeling onions—a soldierly task slightly more distasteful than peeling potatoes—at Camp Kearney, San Diego, California. NARA

Reveille at the U.S. Naval Training Camp in Seattle, Washington. NARA

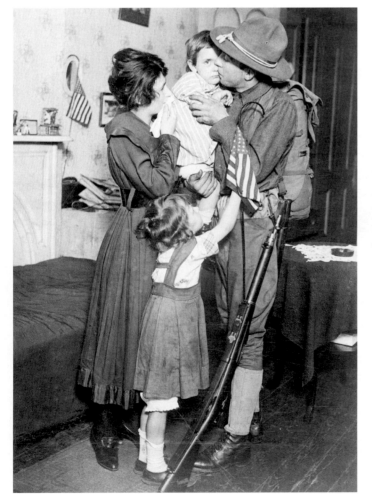

Pvt. Thomas P. Loughlin of B Company, 69th Regiment, New York National Guard, bids his family farewell. The "Fighting 69th" became the 165th Infantry Regiment of the 42nd Division. The historically predominately Irish regiment, commanded by Col. William J. "Wild Bill" Donovan, saw some of the heaviest fighting of the war. Loughlin would be wounded on September 12, 1918, during the St. Mihiel wounded offensive. NARA

The army crossed the Atlantic to France by ship. Here, a group of doughboys embark on the journey. NARA

"Sammies," the European sobriquet for American soldiers, march into Perth, Scotland, to cheering crowds. NARA

A group of U.S. Marines strike a pose for a publicity still entitled "First to Fight." Regrettably for these zealous Marines, the army's 1st Infantry Division would see the first combat action in Europe. NARA

A scene aboard the USS *Texas* shows gobs (sailors) hamming it up for the camera. NARA

A 5-inch gun and its crew onboard an American destroyer. Destroyers were a critical asset for checking the U-boat menace during the voyage across the Atlantic. NARA

Antiaircraft gun practice on a converted yacht being used by the Naval Reserve in California. NARA

The USS *Michigan* underway. NARA

Following individual training in the United States, army units underwent extensive large-unit training overseas. This dramatic photo of a night attack was taken during training maneuvers at the I Corps School, Gondrecourt, France. NARA

This Signal Corps soldier, attached to a cavalry unit, poses at home in Illinois for a studio portrait. (The forty-six-star pattern on the outdated flag in the background predates the admission of New Mexico and Arizona in 1912.) Mounted units would not see significant combat action during the war. PRIVATE COLLECTION

Off to the war, this soldier, simply identified as "Ray," poses with Fern, who appears to be his sister, and Irene, a friend. PRIVATE COLLECTION

In the same studio photo series, Irene and Fern monkey around in army uniforms. Young ladies loved to take comically themed, patriotic photos for the boys going overseas. PRIVATE COLLECTION

A melancholy couple sits for a studio portrait before parting. PRIVATE COLLECTION

Three newly minted soldiers from Fort Oglethorpe or Camp Greenleaf, Georgia, pose on Umbrella Rock, Chattanooga, Tennessee. Umbrella Rock had been a magnet for visitors and accompanying photographers since the Civil War; scores of Civil War soldiers posed on this same rock. PRIVATE COLLECTION

Company C, 308th Machine Gun Battalion, 78th Division, trains at Camp Dix, New Jersey, on a British Vickers machine gun. U.S. troops relied heavily on the Allies for crew-served weapons; the British Vickers was one of the most reliable machine guns of the war. PRIVATE COLLECTION

With their soldier going off to war, every member of the family pitched in to support the war effort. The young girl and her companion prepare to work a victory garden, while the Red Cross member knits. PRIVATE COLLECTION

Pvt. Robert Everett, 122nd Aero Squadron, sent "a picture, but a poor one," to his girl, Claire, from Camp Vail, New Jersey. PRIVATE COLLECTION

Two buddies pose with their sweethearts before heading overseas. PRIVATE COLLECTION

A heavily armed group of gunslingers from Battery B, 81st Field Artillery Regiment, 8th Division, clown for the camera at Camp Doniphan, Fort Sill, Oklahoma, 1918. MHI

Baking bread at Camp Meade, Maryland, 1918. NARA

Recruits drilling at Camp Devens, Massachusetts, 1918. NARA

Training on the Browning Automatic Rifle (BAR), Camp Devens, Massachusetts, 1918. NARA

Two soldiers, identified only as the tallest and shortest recruits at Camp Custer, Michigan, 1917. MHI

Russian master violinist Mischa Elman entertains some soldiers at Camp Kearney, California, in 1918. NARA

Mess time in the field. A soldier enjoys a jelly sandwich at Camp Kearney, California, 1918. NARA

A view of training trenches at Camp Kearney, California, February 1918. NARA

Captain Watson and Lieutenant Carlson of the 103rd Ammunition Train, 28th Division, are visited by their wives and other family members during training at Camp Beauregard, Louisiana. MHI

Men of the 31st Division leave the "Gas House" after training with their gas masks at Camp Wheeler, Georgia. NARA

Sgt. Robert R. Cahal (standing second from left) of Company C, 143rd Infantry Regiment, 36th Division, participates in machine-gun training with the British Lewis Gun at Camp Bowie, Texas, 1918. MHI

Actress Mary Pickford (left) visits with the officers of the 143rd Field Artillery, 40th Division, at Puente, California, in 1918. MHI

Pvt. Hugh F. McGriskin, Company L, 165th
Infantry Regiment, 42nd Division, hams it
up with some lady friends at Camp Mills,
New York. MHI

Army training consisted of toughening up
recruits. The reverse of this photo of
Medical Corps soldiers reads, "Back from a
twenty four mile hike. Tired, but all there."
PRIVATE COLLECTION

A squad of soldiers seem less than happy with their meal arrangements. PRIVATE COLLECTION

Newly Arrived Troops Debarking At Brest by Walter Jack Duncan. CMH

Pvt. (later Sgt.) Merritt H. Bragg, Company A, 317th Infantry Regiment, 80th Division, stands proudly for the photographer at Camp Lee, Petersburg, Virginia. Bragg's unit would see some of the hardest fighting on the Meuse-Argonne, where Bragg miraculously escaped unscathed. PRIVATE COLLECTION

This colorful postcard was typical of greetings sent from home expressing devotion to those serving in arms. PRIVATE COLLECTION

A photo postcard of an unknown soldier has a note from his son inscribed on the reverse: "Can never get used to you being away from me. If I could only be over there with you I believe I'd be happy." PRIVATE COLLECTION

This "Roll Call" postcard was mailed to a female admirer of Loyde Gardner while he was in training at Camp Custer, Michigan. Gardner, soon to be promoted to lieutenant, wrote, "This is a great life, but it doesn't appeal to me." He would serve as an artillery officer in coastal defense batteries along the East Coast, making good his intentions by leaving the army shortly after the Armistice. PRIVATE COLLECTION

CHAPTER 2
THE HUN!

The German Army, the AEF's principal enemy, had three years of combat expertise to draw from. Despite setbacks on the Western Front, the Germans had enjoyed a series of successes, and soldier morale remained high. But as the first American units went into line in France, the German Army was undergoing a series of significant changes, making them a deadlier foe.

Forced by the realities of war, production, and reduced manpower, the German High Command modified overall doctrine on land, at sea, and on the home front. During the period of front-line stabilization in the West (1915–16), German doctrine adhered to a static defense of a massive front and secondary trench line system to be held or retaken at all costs.

The new doctrine incorporated lessons learned from withstanding the attacks on the Somme and their own failed strategy at Verdun. For the moment, Germany had to abandon ideas of advance in the West, take a strategic pause, and wait for the submarine offensive to take effect. As the early advances of 1914 were planned with timetable precision, the new doctrine of defense would be implemented with great efficiency. Between December 1916 and April 1917, the German High Command issued three publications revising the doctrine for the army and in January opened a school to teach the new methods to junior leaders.

Grundsätze für die Führung in der Abwehrschlacht (Principles for the Conduct of the Defensive Battle), published on December 1, 1916, introduced a comprehensive system of defensive tactics for 1917 emphasizing an echelon defense of three basic zones, or battle areas, that was flexible, meaning it could absorb an attack or increase in strength and not break. The concept started with at least three massive belts of heavy-strand barbed wire of the type made to withstand an artillery bombardment.

Along this line, a chain of lightly manned listening/sentry posts would sound the alarm during an attack and provide a limited delaying action while in the process of falling back. The defense would become stronger as the attacker encountered a stiffening response bolstered by machine-gun emplacements, trench mortars, and increasingly larger artillery pieces directed by forward observers.

The second zone would include hardened fixed positions or strongpoint complexes of bunkers and pillboxes encasing machine-gun teams that provided interlocking fire over the areas of approach. These positions were supported by *Eingreif*, or counter-attack battalions.

The third, or rear, battle zone contained larger formations, including machine-gun and artillery units that would concentrate directly on the area of possible breakthrough. These heavy reserves would be committed at the point where most attacks began to weaken and would push the attacking force out of the zone. The depth, up to 9,000 yards in some places, was the key to the overall concept of this type of defense and was based on the observed amount of penetration of previous lines that an Allied attack normally gained.

The defensive manual was supported by two additional important publications in January of 1917. *Allgemeines über Stellenbau* (Principles of Field Position Construction) introduced the method of constructing a new type of defensive position that relied on massive concrete and steel strongpoints from which to anchor these operations, while *Erfahrungen der I Armee in der Sommeschlacht* (Experience of the German First Army in the Somme Battles) explained the reason for the change to the defense-in-depth concept. The manuals stressed that the new lines constructed were to be sited on the reverse slope for maximum defense. During the winter of 1917, the Germans constructed these massive new positions and prepared to fall back to them, a move that would take the Allied armies by surprise.

The defensive concepts replaced men with fortification materiel that needed to be supplied and built. In December 1916, the German High Command initiated the Patriotic Auxiliary Service Law, which mobilized German male citizens between the ages of seventeen and sixty for war production work. The program concentrated production on key strategic materials such as coal, steel, and concrete and attempted to orchestrate increased manufacture of tactical supplies of aircraft, small arms, and artillery munitions. Due to labor factors, political factions, and lack of control over private industrial pricing, wage control, and job allocation, production actually fell during the implementation of the plan. The German people were also suffering from lack of food. By 1917, caloric intake had fallen to an average of 1,000 calories a day. But, despite these obstacles, the new positions were constructed in time for a repositioning in the spring.

THE HINDENBURG LINE

In March, during the preparation phase for the Allied attack scheduled for early April, the Germans produced a surprise of their own. Between March 16 and 20, Operation *Alberich*, named for the evil dwarf character from Wagner's *Niebelung* opera, was put into action by order from Gen. Erich Ludendorff. The German Army withdrew to their newly prepared positions, which became known to the Allies as the Hindenburg Line but in the Arras sector was known to the Germans by its Wagnerian code name, the *Siegfriedstellun*.

The *Alberich* plan was not only a brilliant strategic repositioning that shortened and hardened the German defensive line, but also implemented as a scorched earth policy that destroyed or booby-trapped the landscape and water supplies as the Germans evacuated. Even though the Allies had made great strides in aerial reconnaissance, the Siegfried position was constructed and occupied in secret, a profound failure of Allied intelligence. This move was as devastating to Allied war planning as if the Germans had just produced a smashing offensive victory. Any planned Allied advance in this area would force greater exposure of the troops and require the construction of new positions from which to conduct advances. It also forced an unplanned and costly consumption of material and labor and required intelligence-gathering and reconnaissance of the new positions to assess strongpoints and assign targets. For up to 30 miles in some sections there was nothing but an abandoned, shell-holed no-man's-land without roads, bridges, rail lines, or buildings—a landscape poisoned, booby-trapped, and stripped bare of anything of material use. Whole villages were destroyed, the populations relocated and forced to work in the rear areas.

In total, the German Army constructed five major defensive lines, which ran from the northern coast down to the Meuse-Argonne sector in the south:

- *Wotan Stellung* (position) stretched from the Belgian coast to Cambrai
- *Siegfried Stellung* stretched from Cambrai to St. Quentin
- *Alberich Stellung* stretched from St. Quentin to Laon
- *Brunhilde Stellung* stretched from Laon across the Champagne front
- *Kriemhilde Stellung* stretched from the Argonne Forest to Metz

THE YANKS ARE COMING!

"America from a military stand point means nothing" stated Adm. Eduard von Capelle, the German secretary of state for the navy, in a January address to the German *Reichstag* (parliament). Viewing the situation in early 1918, with only six infantry divisions partially constituted in France, he may have been correct in his assumption. As hundreds of thousands of men underwent rudimentary military training in forty-four divisional organizations in the United States, the basic question of getting them to France in time to make an impact was of great concern. There simply wasn't enough equipment to outfit them or the ships to do the job. Capelle even boasted that the Americans would never even make it across the Atlantic, a reference to intended German submarine operations.

To efficiently use the number of ships available and save time, Pershing and the Allies developed a plan that would emphasize getting the men over with their basic equipment first and rely on French and British industry to provide the artillery, transport, tanks, aircraft, and other required munitions of trench warfare to be manned by the AEF. Another issue that had to be overcome was where to land the anticipated influx of men and materiel. Northern French ports were already overloaded with cross-channel traffic. The ports on the French western and southern coasts were less congested and would be built up, along with rail networks, to support the training, supply, and deployment of AEF units in a distinct American zone that the Allies agreed would eventually be turned over to a proposed American army organization. The original zone selected for the AEF placed them south of Verdun on the Meuse River, starting on a bend in the approximately fifty-mile trench line at St. Mihiel and running northeast to Pont-à-Mousson astride the Moselle River. This zone would expand as the AEF grew and became part of the Allied advance.

AEF TRAINING AND SUPPLY

Once in France, the American troops had to undergo a great deal of training, which included everything from basic sanitation, to small and large combined arms operations, to staff work. Specialized schools were established all over France to teach everything from throwing a grenade, to baking large amounts of bread, to planning, supplying, and executing artillery barrages. New organizations were developed from scratch with French- and British-supplied equipment, including an Army Air

Service and the Tank Corps. Another organization that would be developed was the Services of Supply, an enormous logistical organization that handled everything from beans to artillery shells. For every three soldiers in the AEF, one soldier served in a support organization, which in turn was augmented by 23,772 civilians.

On average, the forty-three American divisions sent to France would spend eight months in training before being placed in the line. Officers were routinely absent from their immediate units, receiving weeks of specialized schooling. But in training and doctrine, the AEF was a conflicted organization. Pershing mistrusted European methods and had come to view the prolonged and costly situation on the Western Front as a result of addiction to trench warfare and its specialized weapons. He believed in the primacy of the infantryman and his rifle to win the battle in the open. So while his men were trained in French methods, his offensive plans would throw them into the open, advancing in line against hardened German emplacements in attacks reminiscent of the campaigns in 1914–16. The result was reckless and predictable.

1918

After negotiating a separate peace with the extremist revolutionary government in Russia on March 3, 1918, the German High Command raced to transfer fifty divisions from the Eastern Front to the West, bringing the German Army's strength up to over 3.5 million men, arranged in 194 divisions. General Ludendorff readied the German Army to convert from defensive to offensive operations in a bid to force the Allies to negotiate a peace before the weight of the American effort would tip the balance. He planned to attack on the Somme, split the British Army from the French, and push it into the sea. Meanwhile, the Allied governments entered negotiations once again on how to best prosecute the war. The Lloyd-George government wanted to hold the line on the Western Front but attack the Central Powers elsewhere and suggested the reduction of Turkish forces. The Allies, now with America added to the mix, still did not have a plan for common action or centralized control. Events would quickly demand a remedy.

FRIEDENSTURM

Like the elastic defense-in-depth doctrine employed in 1917 that completely frustrated the Allies, the Germans would unleash a new "offensive-in-depth" doctrine in the spring of 1918 that used the same formations, in reverse, on the attack. Previously, the British had concentrated on converging fire and

assault forces to hammer through a limited section of the defensive line. The new German assault tactics concentrated on selectively choosing what and where to engage during an attack, bypassing strongpoints and focusing on getting into the rear area and destroying artillery, communication, and reinforcement centers as quickly as possible. This was a refinement of Russian general Aleksei Alekseevich Brusilov's concepts of fingerlike formations of infantry infiltration and fast artillery bombardment demonstrated in 1916. The new tactics, first tried against the Russians at Riga on September 3 and at the Italian battle of Caporetto on October 21, 1917, sent forward small, fast-moving assault groups after a short bombardment, followed by artillery fire of high-explosive rounds mixed with chemical shells of various types of gas and smoke on selected communication, reserve, and supply points in the rear.

On March 21, 1918, the German Seventeenth, Second, and Eighteenth Armies used the new concepts and drove 40 miles into the British lines, destroying Gen. Sir Hubert de la Poer Gough's British Fifth Army. The Germans captured over 80,000 men and 975 artillery pieces, as well as key bridges over the Somme River. The bulge in the line ran all the way from Arras in the north, with its apex centering on Cantigny, then bent back to Barisis in the south. Two days later, on March 23 at 7:20 A.M., Paris came under artillery attack, for the first time during the war, from three massive long-range guns that would hold the City of Lights in terror until August, claim the lives of 256 people, and leave another 620 wounded. By March 25, Haig informed the French that unless he received help, he would have to consider withdrawal to the Channel ports, and the coalition forces would be split.

With the goal of destroying the BEF, Ludendorff turned his eye to the northern positions around Flanders and ordered the Fourth Army to attack Plumer's British Second Army at Wytschaete and Messines, south of Ypres; and the German Sixth Army to attack the British First Army under Horne that held the line between Armentières and Givenchy. In what has become known as the Lys Offensive, or the Second German Drive, which struck on April 9, Plumer and Horne fell back but offered stiff resistance. In the middle of these hurricane assaults, Haig issued a direct statement to the troops, declaring that the British were fighting with their "backs to the wall" and must draw upon the "justice of their cause" to defend to the last man. The British resistance stiffened, and the German gains were contained to a 13-mile-deep penetration along the East–West Hazebrouck to Armentières railway near

Strazeele. By April 29, the drive had been stopped, but more was to come.

While these events unfolded, Haig called for a meeting of the Allies to discuss the situation; as a result, on April 14, Marshall Ferdinand Foch was named Allied commander in chief to create a staff organization to direct all Allied actions against the Central Powers. Foch came to the job with a three-point plan he would soon put into action and began to organize a strong Allied defense as well as offensive operations. To strengthen the British position, Gen. Sir Henry Seymour Rawlinson replaced Gough as commander of the Fifth Army, which was finally bolstered by 75,000 men in three divisions sent over from England.

On April 23, the British navy launched a raid on the Belgian port of Zeebrugge, whose main channel was a major outlet for German submarines. Although it did not all go off as planned, the Royal Navy was able sink two "block" ships filled with concrete at the narrowest point in the channel and detonate two submarines filled with explosives against the viaduct in an attempt to wreck the port.

THE GERMAN DRIVE TO THE SOUTH

Under strict secrecy, Ludendorff amassed an assault force of 41 divisions and 1,036 heavy guns in the forest south of Laon. The night before the attack, two German soldiers captured in the area of the old Chemin Des Dames battlefield told of an impending major offensive in the area, but it was too late to prepare. At 1:00 A.M. on May 27, the German artillery unleashed a bombardment that reached back 12 miles into the French reserve and artillery line, smothering the area in exploding steel. Under complete darkness at 3:40 in the morning, seventeen assault divisions moved south, and the French Sixth Army under Gen. Denis Auguste Duchêne dissolved.

Events for the tiny AEF began to move rapidly. On March 28, General Pershing and Gen. Tasker Bliss met with Foch and offered the immediate use of all manpower the AEF had in France for the emergency. That very day, the U.S. 1st Infantry Division, under the support of the French Army, successfully assaulted the town of Cantigny, the first objective taken by an AEF infantry division. On the morning of May 29, the Germans captured Soissons, and the French government began to make preparations to evacuate from Paris to Bordeaux. The German forces drove on to the River Marne, 37 miles from Paris, reaching Château-Thierry on June 1. Here, the 7th Machine Gun Battalion of the U.S. 3rd Infantry Division manned the bridges with French Hotchkiss machine guns and stopped the attackers on June 2.

Farther west, the French Sixth Army, bolstered by the U.S. 2nd Division, was determined to stop the German drive to Paris. The 2nd Infantry Division was unique in that it contained a brigade of Marines who attacked the German positions north of Lucy-le-Bocage in a forest known as the Belleau Wood. The Marines' ferocious attacks, launched into the wood between June 6 and June 25, blunted the German drive on Paris.

The Germans had advanced 34 miles, penetrating deep into French lines along a 55-mile front in nine days, but had completely outrun their supply lines. In seventy-six whirlwind days, the German Army had erased all the hard-fought gains since 1916.

Like a boxer, Ludendorff struck the French left on June 9 between Montdidier and Noyon on the Oise River. After two days, the German advance was stopped by a Franco-American defense. Foch issued a document on June 16 instructing all Allied commanders to create defense-in-depth positions to counter the German tactics used on the drives. He also issued plans for three counteroffensives on Lys, the Somme, and the Marne.

THE SPANISH FLU

The end of June and early July did not produce any major offensive actions as both sides consolidated supplies and men, but now nature would take up the war on its own. In the early spring, French soldiers complained about a flu that lasted about three days. By March, cases had been diagnosed in the United States, and it spread worldwide at an alarming rate. In Germany, the malnourished population suffered acutely from the flu and reduced its capacity to continue the war. At the time, it was reported that 21.5 million people died from the flu worldwide, although by more accurate postwar reporting, totals may well have exceeded 50 million.

CHAMPAGNE–MARNE OFFENSIVE

With the German forces resupplied, orders were issued to push the German Seventh and First Armies south against the Marne, enveloping the fortified city of Reims. Due to accurate intelligence, the French knew the location, date, and hour of attack. The U.S. 3rd Infantry Division was added to the French Center Army group and moved up to the Marne River. To counter the attack, the French launched a preemptive bombardment and caught many of the German assault units before they could advance.

On the left of the Allied line, the German 10th Infantry Division, rated as a first-class assault unit, crossed the Marne between Château-Thierry and a small bridge and farm near the town of Mézy. This section of the river was held in force by the 30th Infantry Regiment, U.S. 3rd Infantry Division. Numbering 3,700 strong, this one regiment contained more men than the whole French division to which it was assigned.

The Germans locked horns with the men of the 30th Infantry but were thrown back. During the attack, the French units on the 3rd's right and left flanks fell back to keep the infantry out of the German bombardment and to allow the French artillery to stop the advance, but this plan was not clearly communicated and left the Yanks on their own in their first battle. Fighting in small groups in an area of 3 square miles, the 3rd Infantry division inflicted 400 German casualties and held fast, earning the distinction of "Rock of the Marne." Little did they know at the time, their actions would prove to be a turning point in the war.

With the Germans checked on the Marne, Foch ordered a counterattack for July 18. Eight U.S. infantry divisions took part in the offensive supporting the French Tenth, Sixth, Ninth, and Fifth Armies. To lead it off, the French Tenth Army under Gen. Charles Mangin unleashed a surprise attack supported by the 1st and 2nd U.S. Infantry Divisions and parts of the 4th. The Allies pushed hard against a skillful German withdrawal that was covered by ample machine guns and screening artillery bombardments. In ten days, the Germans had fallen back 12 miles to the Ourcq River, and by August 6, the line had been pushed another 10 miles to the River Vesle, retaking Soissons and reducing the threat to Paris. Unknown to the Allies at the time, Foch's counterattack took the initiative and forced Ludendorff on July 20 to cancel his planned attack on Haig's forces. The BEF had been spared.

On July 24, Foch met with Haig and Pershing and laid out plans for a series of bold offensives, as many of the German units had spent their strength and come out of their hardened defenses with their supply lines overextended. Foch proposed a shift to the BEF zone of operations. During the German drive, the important north–south rail junction at Montdidier had been taken; this had to be freed for logistical purposes. Ludendorff did not expect an attack between Arras and Amiens, thinking any British effort would be around Ypres.

After careful and secret preparations, at 4:20 A.M. on August 8, Haig reprised the artillery-tank-aircraft strategy of Cambrai and unleashed a crashing, rolling barrage followed by 400 tanks, including some of the new Whippet models that had entered the line in March. The Whippets, which could move at approximately 6 miles an hour, were intended to fill the role

the cavalry could not accomplish at Cambrai; one named Musical Box did just that, shooting up the German rear area for eleven hours. After the first day, 1,700 Allied aircraft dominated the battlefield. The attack was a complete rout bagging 15,000 prisoners and 400 artillery pieces, and driving in 9 miles on the first day. It was noted that German defensive operations were confused. The offensive, which lasted until September 2, caused Ludendorff to order two successive withdrawals, stopping his line before St. Quentin. The Germans had lost another 100,000 men, and morale ebbed away.

U.S. FIRST ARMY ACTIVATED

While the Germans were suffering reversals at the hands of the BEF, Marshall Foch authorized General Pershing to activate the U.S. First Army on August 10. The Foch–Pershing agreement to create an independent army came with conditions that would truly test the new organization. The agreed plan would have the First Army reduce the St. Mihiel sector bulge; stabilize the line; create an American Second Army using newly arrived divisions; disengage First Army from battle; move its 600,000 men, 3,000 artillery pieces, and supplies approximately 50 miles over three main roads into the Meuse-Argonne sector; and be ready for renewed action in a matter of fourteen days. It was a very tough timetable even for a mature organization, and when Pershing left Foch's headquarters, French staff officers expressed doubts they would pull it off.

Pershing turned to a young colonel on his staff by the name of George C. Marshall and entrusted him with the monumental task of creating the operational order for the largest logistical move in army history. Marshall created the plan in an hour while poring over a map of the area. On September 12, 1918, the U.S. First Army launched an offensive of its own, opening with a heavy bombardment at 1:00 A.M. After four hours of artillery bombardment, men of nine American divisions and three French Colonial Corps cleared the St. Mihiel salient in thirty-six hours, capturing 15,000 men and 250 guns.

The attacking infantry were supported by Col. William "Billy" Mitchell's ad-hoc air force of 600 planes, flown by pilots from five different Allied countries who executed a complex air-support plan that devastated the Germans. Roaring to life for the first time in combat, the AEF Tank Corps employed French FT-17 tanks under the command of Lt. Co. George Patton, who was wounded in the attack. Pershing's First Army was a success and advanced over 12 miles along a nearly 50-mile front. Immediately, Marshall's plan was put into action, and heavy artillery units began to reposition for the long march north. The move was rough-and-tumble, with poor weather and road conditions, traffic jams, and broken-down transport, but it did go off successfully and on time.

On September 20, the American Second Army was activated under Gen. Robert L. Bullard and took over the new St. Mihiel sector line. Pershing and the AEF now had responsibility for an approximately 80-mile section of the front, with the rough terrain around Verdun and the Argonne Forest held by General Gallwitz's German Army in a 12-mile-deep defensive position ahead of him.

THE ALLIED DRIVE

With the numerical superiority and the AEF in place in front of the Argonne Forest, Foch was ready to launch the whole of the Allied line at once. Their main objective was to deny the enemy the use of the railroad centers at Aulnoye and Mézières outside of Sedan.

On September 26, the Franco-American offensive against the Meuse-Argonne sector crashed into the forest. From September 27 to 29, the Allies launched one offensive operation per day from the Argonne to the Ypres salient. All along the line, the Germans began to retreat. By October 3, the German High Command began talking seriously about entering into peace negotiations while pulling their armies back to keep them intact. The Germans gave ground stubbornly, leaving pockets of machine-gun crews and artillery to slow down the advancing Allied forces and exacting high numbers of casualties. The action moved from open warfare to trenches and strongpoints and back again. There was little chance for maneuver, and the U.S. infantry divisions suffered high losses while battering the German defenders.

On October 12, Prince Max of the German state of Baden contacted the government of the United States with the message that the German High Command wanted to negotiate terms. This set off a series of military and diplomatic events that would bring the war to an end.

On October 18, the AEF broke through the defense system in the Argonne, and the British drive in the north took Le Cateau, heading toward the railhead at Aulnoye. It was too much for General Ludendorff, who resigned on October 27. The next day, the German navy mutinied. On November 1, the U.S. First Army, now commanded by Gen. Hunter Liggett, rammed its way to Boult-aux-Bois, and in five days the U.S. 42nd Infantry Division was before the city of Sedan. Events moved at a rapid but deadly pace.

The Allies finally determined the language of the armistice agreement that would be presented to the Germans on November 4, and on November 6 around midnight, Marshall Foch received a wireless message that German delegates wanted to cross the lines.

On November 9, a German republic was proclaimed, and on November 10, the same day the U.S. Second Army broke through in their sector, the Kaiser abdicated his throne. An end was in sight.

SILENCE

Due to the nature of the negotiations, which were centered on the concept of an armistice, or cessation of hostilities, and a fear that the arrangement would not hold for a real peace (it had not on two prior occasions with the Bolshevik Russians on the Eastern Front), each side fought until the very last moment on November 11, the day the war would cease. With guns roaring out to the last second, every soldier held his breath for the eleventh hour and the eleventh minute.

When it came, the guns fell silent and it was over. Troops leapt out of the trenches in celebration; unfortunately, quite a number were killed, as some units did not receive word that the war had ended. The Allies would dig in and wait until November 17, when Marshall Foch issued orders to advance and reoccupy all territory once held by the enemy, a task completed on November 30. As per the agreement, Allied troops crossed the Rhine bridgeheads into Germany for occupation duty on December 1. The original armistice terms lasted for a brief period of thirty-six days and were followed by formal negotiations that would begin in earnest.

Gen. John J. Pershing was designated to command the newly created American Expeditionary Force. LOC

French Prime Minister Georges Clemenceau and General Pershing review the Guard of Honor at AEF General Headquarters, Chaumont, France, June 23, 1918. NARA

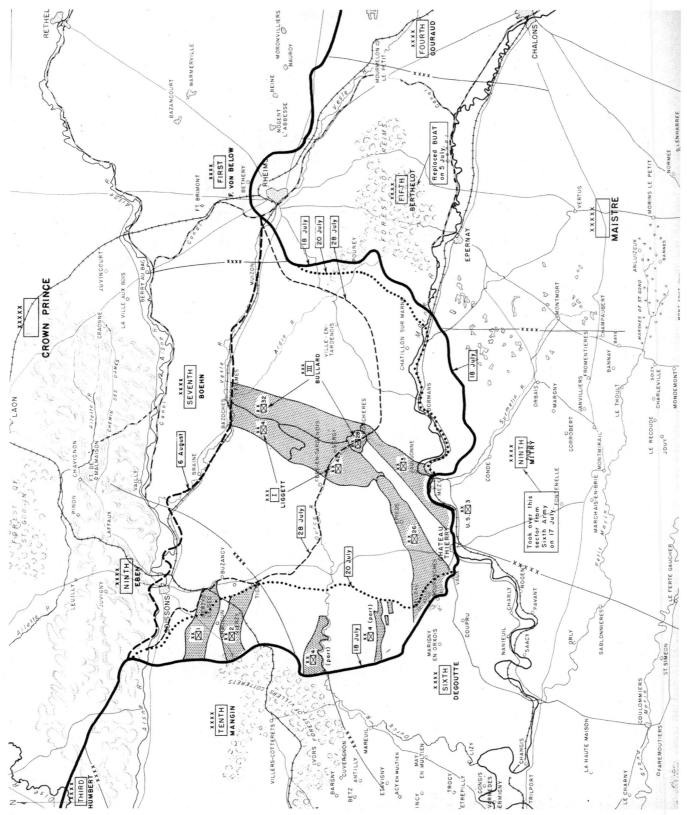

By the time an operational American army arrived in France, the Germans had once again threatened the last material obstacle between them and Paris: the Marne River. CMH

German general Erich Ludendorff's (right) Peace Offensive was designed to split the French and British Allied forces and force a truce before American troops could arrive in France in sufficient numbers to conduct offensive operations. LOC

At German General Headquarters, General von Hindenburg (left) confers with Kaiser Wilhelm (center) and General Ludendorff (right). LOC

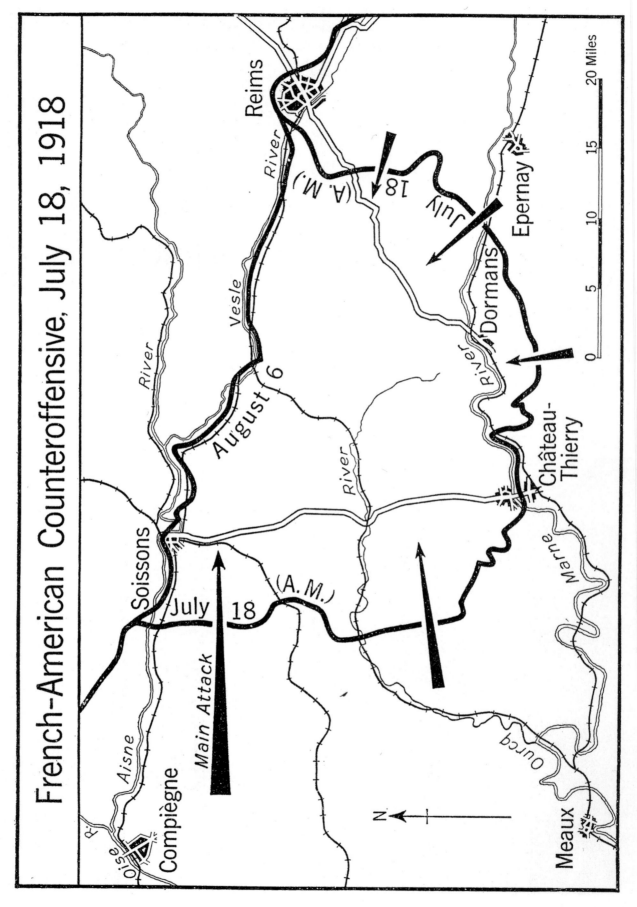

French-American Counteroffensive, July 18, 1918

Franco-American operations initially focused on reduction of the Marne salient. ABMC

American troops operating a French "37" in a firing position on a parapet in a second-line trench. The gun had a maximum range of 1.5 miles, was more accurate than a rifle, and was capable of firing twenty-eight rounds per minute. NARA

African-American officers of the 92nd Division "Buffalos" in France with a young admirer. Activists in the African-American community successfully lobbied to get commissioned officers into the Army officer corps. NARA

African-American troops of the 369th Infantry Regiment "Harlem Hellfighters," 93rd Division, in formation. Detached to the French as a direct result of the prevailing prejudice against "colored" soldiers fighting alongside whites, the regiment proved fearless in combat. NARA

Snipers of the 166th Infantry Regiment, 42nd Division, in a nest pick off Germans on the outer edge of Villers-sur-Fère, France. NARA

Sharpshooters of the 28th Infantry Regiment, 1st Division, use an old brick wall as cover in Bonvillers, France. NARA

Lt. Col. R. D. Garrett, chief signal officer, 42nd Division, tests a telephone left behind by the Germans in hasty retreat from the St. Mihiel salient, Essey, France. NARA

AEF soldiers using the observation instruments left behind at the Crown Prince's bunker after the hasty German retreat from the Marne. NARA

An army gun crew from the Regimental Headquarters Company, 23rd Infantry Regiment, 2nd Division, fires a 37mm gun during the advance against the Germans in Belleau Wood near Château-Thierry, France. NARA

An antiaircraft machine gun of the 101st Field Artillery Regiment, 26th Division, fires on a German observation plane at Chemin des Dames, France. NARA

Battery C, 6th Field Artillery Regiment, 1st Infantry Division, fired the first shot for the United States on the Lorraine front. This image captures the moment of the shot; note the shell casing flying through the air and a new shell sliding into the breech, occurring in the same fraction of a second. NARA

Men of the 35th Coast Artillery Regiment load a 13.9-inch mobile railroad gun on the Argonne front. Coast artillery regiments, normally devoted to the defense of the United States coastline, were deployed to France to man large-caliber artillery. NARA

FT-17 French Renault tanks were widely used by the AEF. Here, Americans move forward along the Meuse-Argonne front. NARA

The commander and gunner of a British Whippet tank (with hatches open) were among the American tankers northwest of Verdun. NARA

The tenacious defense of the Marne River crossing by the 3rd Division's ("Rock of the Marne") machine-gun battalion averted disaster for the Allies. Here, a machine gun of Company A, 9th Machine Gun Battalion, is set up in a railroad shop at Château-Thierry, France. NARA

President Wilson directed that one infantry regiment, the 332nd Infantry, be sent to the Italian front to bolster the morale of his Italian allies. In this photo, members of the regiment hurl hand grenades into the Austrian trenches. NARA

French troops assault a German position. This photo clearly illustrates the problem of open maneuver on the Western Front: The German Army learned how to make every wrinkle in the ground into a formidable defensive position. NARA

This photo was staged for educational purposes but still conveys the lethality of chemical warfare. Chemical munitions accounted for an estimated 1,296,853 casualties during the war. The man grasping his throat is Maj. Evarts Tracy of the Engineer Corps, a noted instructor at the Engineer School, Langres, France. Evarts survived the war but died in France in 1922 of heart disease. NARA

Gas masks were required for both men and animals; in this photo, a man fits his horse with a mask. As with most specialty equipment needed at the front, American troops relied on their allies, using the British Small Box Respirator or the French Mark 2 gas masks until American production could ramp up. NARA

The Machine Gun Company, 18th Infantry Regiment, 1st Infantry Division, passes through St. Baussant advancing on the St. Mihiel front. NARA

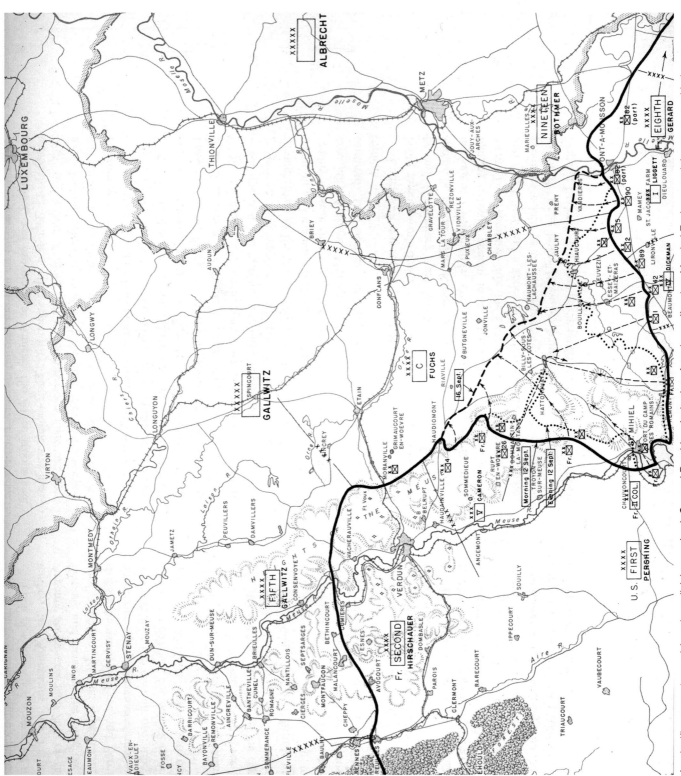

As significant numbers of American divisions arrived, General Pershing desired an American offensive. Marshal Foch granted the request, with the caveat that the St. Mihiel salient be reduced first. CMH

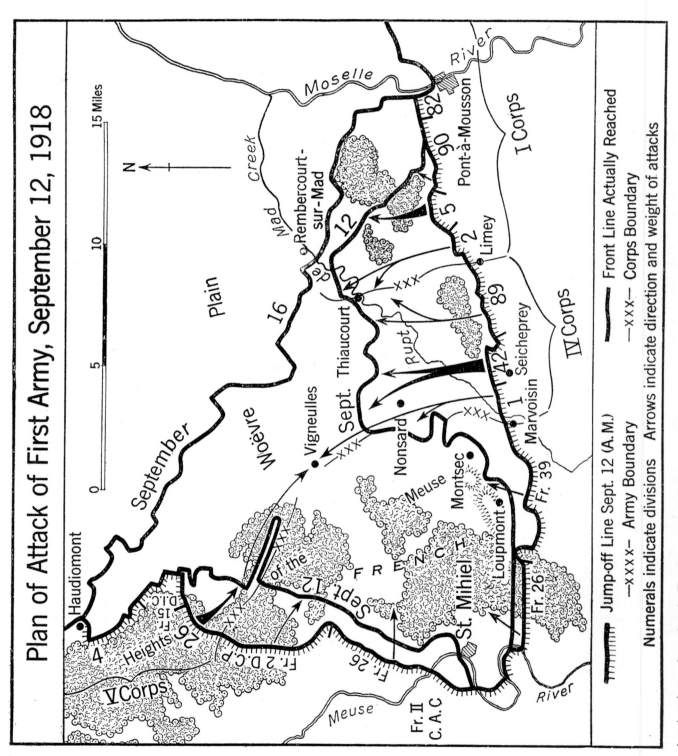

Plan of Attack of First Army, September 12, 1918

American forces, formed as the First Army, would attack the St. Mihiel salient from the south, pinching off the bulge, as French forces attacked from the northwest, forcing a general German withdrawal. ABMC

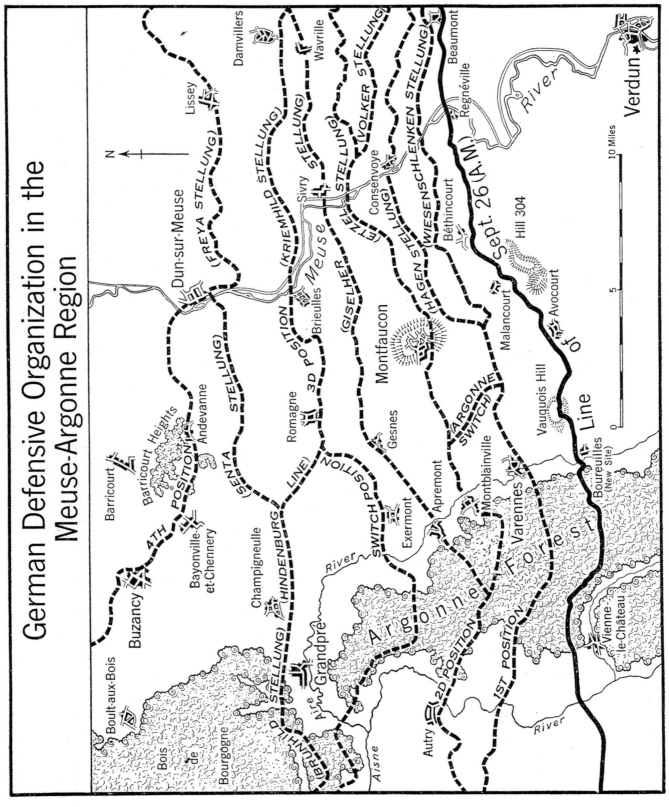

German Defensive Organization in the Meuse-Argonne Region

After the reduction of the St. Mihiel salient, the AEF would relocate 60 miles north to the Meuse-Argonne and attempt to break the Hindenburg Line. German defenses were seemingly impregnable, with endless strongpoints, switchbacks, and depth. ABMC

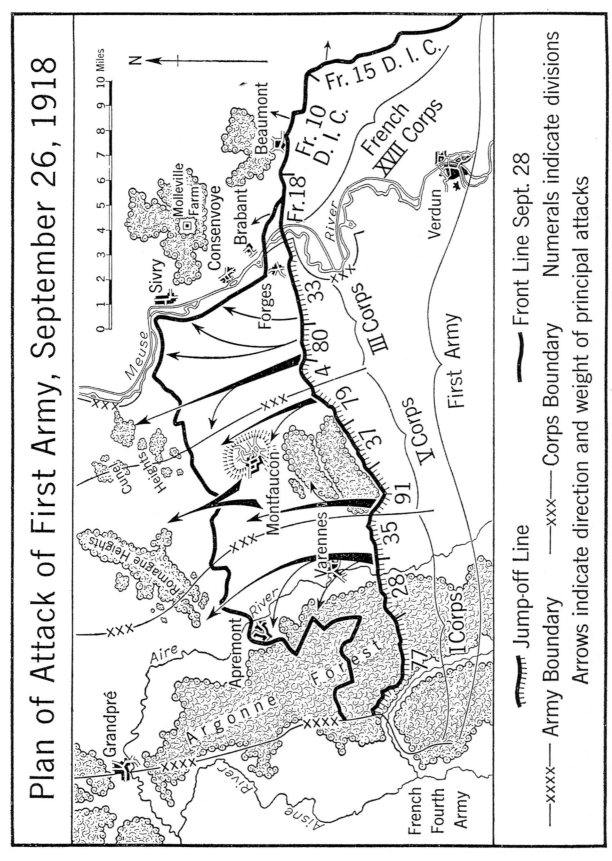

Plan of Attack of First Army, September 26, 1918

The object of the Meuse-Argonne campaign was the lateral railroad line, which supplied the German Army, located just behind the Hindenburg Line at Sedan. The plan for the attack called for a general assault across a wide front, with the Argonne Forest on the left and the Meuse River on the right. ABMC

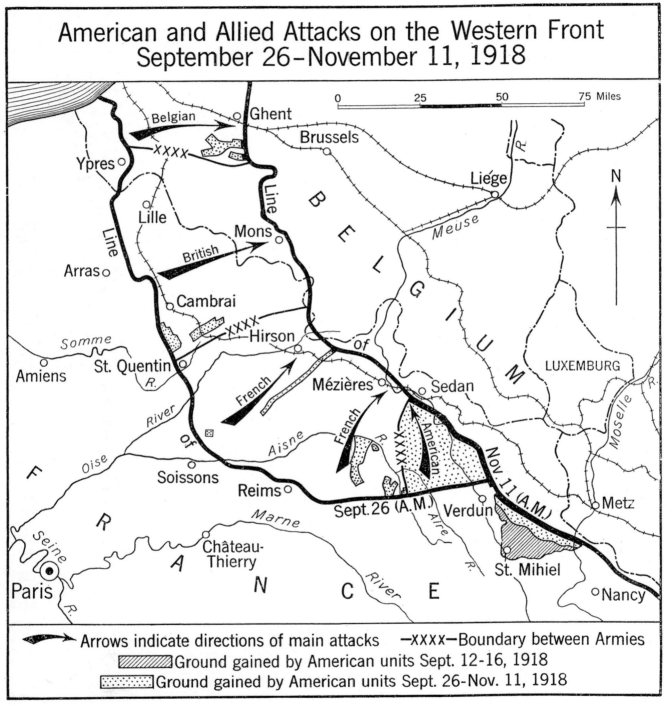

American and Allied Attacks on the Western Front September 26–November 11, 1918

The AEF II Corps, detached to the British north of St. Quentin, conducted a series of operations simultaneously to prevent German forces from relocating along the front. ABMC

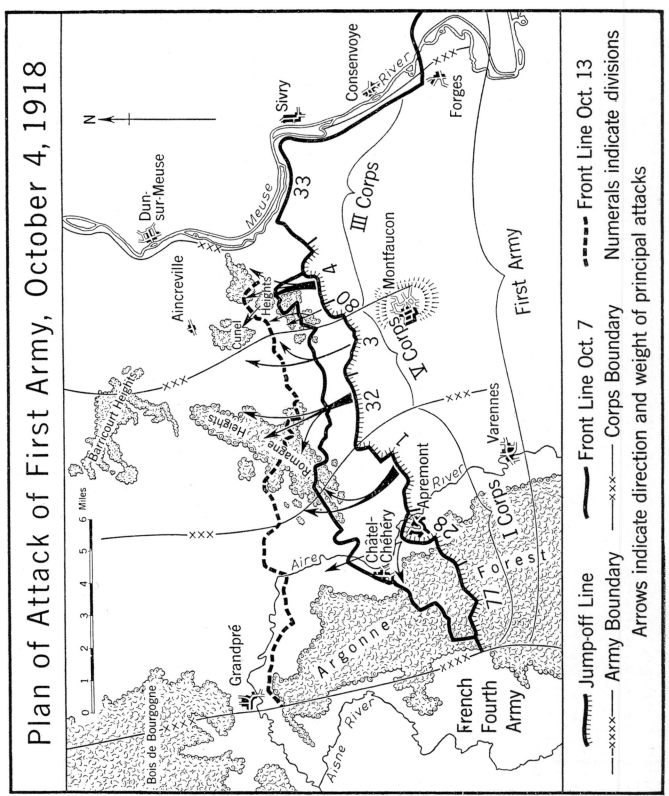

Plan of Attack of First Army, October 4, 1918

By the beginning of October—at great cost—the first and second German Hindenburg defensive positions had fallen; the AEF was making progress. ABMC

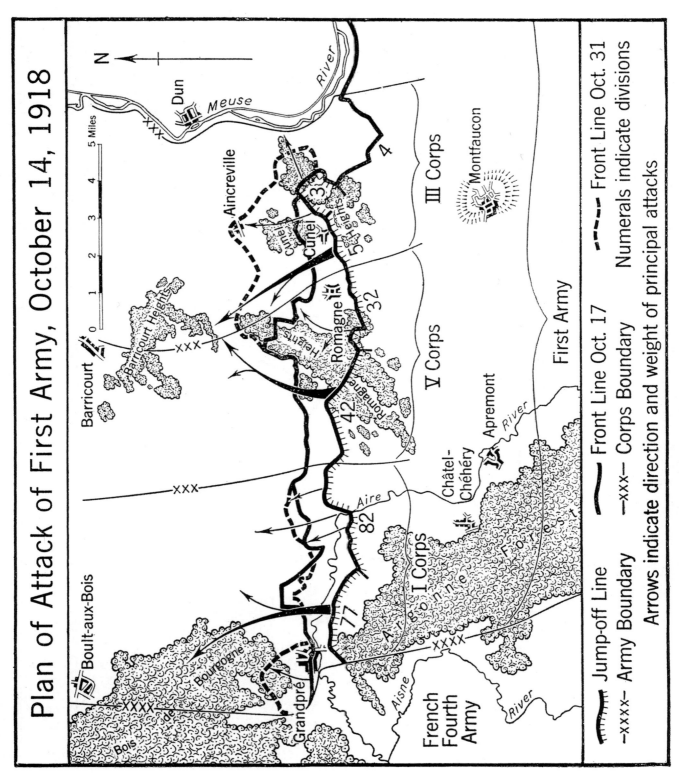

Plan of Attack of First Army, October 14, 1918

First Army planned its final assault on the Hindenburg Line by the middle of the month. ABMC

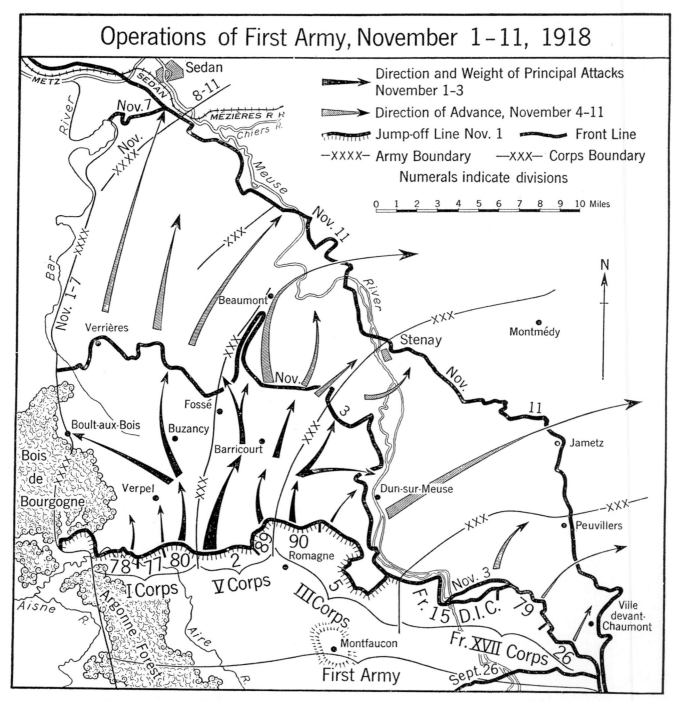

Operations of First Army, November 1–11, 1918

Legend:
- ➤ Direction and Weight of Principal Attacks November 1–3
- ➤ Direction of Advance, November 4–11
- Jump-off Line Nov. 1
- Front Line
- –XXXX– Army Boundary
- –XXX– Corps Boundary
- Numerals indicate divisions

0 1 2 3 4 5 6 7 8 9 10 Miles

The collapse of the Hindenburg Line marked the end of effective German military operations. ABMC

Ouilla Polker of the 1st Engineers, 1st Division, wears a Boche (German) leather helmet taken from a prisoner at Seichepray, Meurthe-et-Moselle, France, September 12, 1918. NARA

This old wagon wheel makes a solid revolving base for a Hotchkiss antiaircraft gun belonging to a squad of Battery E, 6th Field Artillery, 1st Division, at Ménil-la-Tour, France. NARA

Major General Hines, commander of the III Corps, awards the Distinguished Service Medal to Col. Hugh B. Myers, chief of staff, 2nd Division in Engers, Germany, June 1919. NARA

American soldier of Company E, 39th Infantry Regiment, 4th Division, looking over an old monument on the Rhine erected in honor of the Prussian victory over the French in 1871. NARA

Infantrymen of the 4th Division escort German prisoners to the rear near Montreuil-aux-Lions, France, July 1918. NARA

Pvt. Karl D. Eaton, Company K, 59th Infantry Regiment, 4th Division, shows off his field equipment. PRIVATE COLLECTION

Three pals from the 6th Infantry Regiment, 5th Division—from left to right: P. McCourdy, Sam Kreig, and Dennis Wright—mug for the camera. MHI

"Stubby," the 26th "Yankee" Division's mascot, was a Boston Bull Terrier who went overseas with the division. He was a veteran of six fronts and was wounded in action at Seicheprey on April 20, 1918. His preserved body is on display at the Smithsonian's National Museum of American History, Washington, D.C. NARA

A view of the field headquarters of the 26th Division in the Château-Thierry sector as they pursued the Germans in the Marne. From left to right: 1st Lt. Edwin Cooper; Maj. Gen. Clarence Edwards, the division commander; and Col. Duncan K. Major, the division's chief of staff. NARA

Dr. Morton Price, a Massachusetts state representative, talks with men of the 26th Division in August 1918. NARA

Men of the 105th Machine Gun Battalion, 27th Division, fall in after a night's rest at St. Souplet. NARA

Edwin F. Meyer shot this photo of the mess of B Company, 107th Field Signal Battalion, 32nd Division, near Montfaucon in the Argonne Forest. MHI

Maj. Gen. Peter Traub, 35th Division commander (left), speaks with Maj. S. C. Cordiner, 60th Coast Artillery Corps, at 35th Division headquarters near Boureuilles, France, in September 1918. NARA

The 37th Division commander, Maj. Gen. Charles S. Farnsworth, in the Bois de Récicourt, France, September 1918. NARA

Members of the 119th Infantry Regiment, 30th Division, help a little Belgian boy carry his burden home in the Watou area of Belgium, July 8, 1918. The 30th and 27th Divisions fought with the British Expeditionary Force. NARA

Soldiers of the 145th Field Artillery Regiment, 40th Division, in France, October 1918, clean the mud and rust from shells before firing. NARA

Pvt. Dewey A. Teall snapped this photo of men of Battery C, 147th Field Artillery Regiment, 37th Division, engaged in a "cootie hunt" in France, 1918. MHI

Col. William J. "Wild Bill" Donovan (left), commander of the 165th Infantry Regiment, 42nd Division, poses with Chaplain Francis P. Duffy in Remagen, Germany, May 1919. NARA

Maj. Charles Whittlesey (right), commander of the 308th Infantry Regiment, 77th Division, the "Lost Battalion," confers with Major Kenny of the 307th Infantry Regiment near Apremont, France, October 29, 1918. Kenny's 3rd Battalion was the first to relieve Whittlesey's men. The story of the "Lost Battalion" became one of the great heroic episodes of the war. NARA

Survivors of the "Lost Battalion" pose after their relief near Apremont, France, in 1918. Major Whittlesey is standing on the far left. NARA

One of the indelible memories many World War I veterans had was of the ride on a French "40 and 8" railcar. Here, soldiers of Company E, 336th Infantry Regiment, 84th Division, board trains to the front as replacements in Monpont, France, October 1918. NARA

The men and guns of Battery E, 342nd Field Artillery Regiment, 89th Division, France, 1918. NARA

Noncommissioned officers of the 92nd Division at bayonet training, I Corps School, Gondrecourt, France, August 1918. NARA

An artilleryman writes a letter home in the doorway of his splinter-proof shelter on March 7, 1918. NARA

First Lt. George F. Jonaitis, Catholic chaplain of the 313th Infantry Regiment, 79th Division, at the Regimental Command Post, Bois de l'Hôpital, St. Hippolyte, Tryon, Meuse, France, October 14, 1918. NARA

Lt. Col. George Florence, 166th Infantry Regiment; Maj. R. C. Allen, 165th Infantry Regiment, 42nd Division; and staff leaving dugout inspection of the front lines at Blémerey, France. NARA

Pioneer Platoon, Headquarters Company, 164th Infantry Regiment, 41st Division, and some of their equipment for laying barbed-wire entanglements, seen at I Corps School, Gondrecourt, France, August 16, 1918. NARA

Sgt. Alvin C. York, 328th Infantry Regiment, 82nd Division, who, with the aid of his squad, captured 132 German prisoners in the Argonne Forest. He is shown here near the site of the action that earned him the Medal of Honor. NARA

Bystander copyright. **WHAT IT REALLY FEELS LIKE**
To be on patrol duty at night-time.

A comic postcard for the folks at home explains the feeling a new soldier has alone and out on patrol for the first time. Disembodied heads of Germans swirl around in the darkness, scaring the poor soldier to death. PRIVATE COLLECTION

Capt. C. L. Bricka consults a map with soldiers on the road to Chatel-Chéhéry as an accompanying horse takes some equine interest in their destination. NARA

What every doughboy thought about (and hoped) on the front.

PRIVATE COLLECTION

Crossing the Pontoon Bridge, Château-Thierry by William James Aylward. CMH

During the American advance southwest of Verdun, an officer stands at the ruined church on the crest of the captured height of Montfaucon. This was the condition of the site after the Americans finally drove out the Germans. NARA

Surviving officers of the 6th Regiment, 2nd Battalion, U.S. Marines, at Belleau Wood, France. MCHC

Marines at Château-Thierry. MCHC

"Big Nims" with gas mask during a drill, 366th Infantry, 92nd Division, Ainvelle, Vosges, France. NARA

A detachment of the 369th Infantry Regiment, 93rd Division, in the trenches in France. NARA

A young recruit poses in front of an American flag, answering the call of his country. MHI

The face of this unidentified soldier in a French portrait shows the unmistakable mark of war. MHI

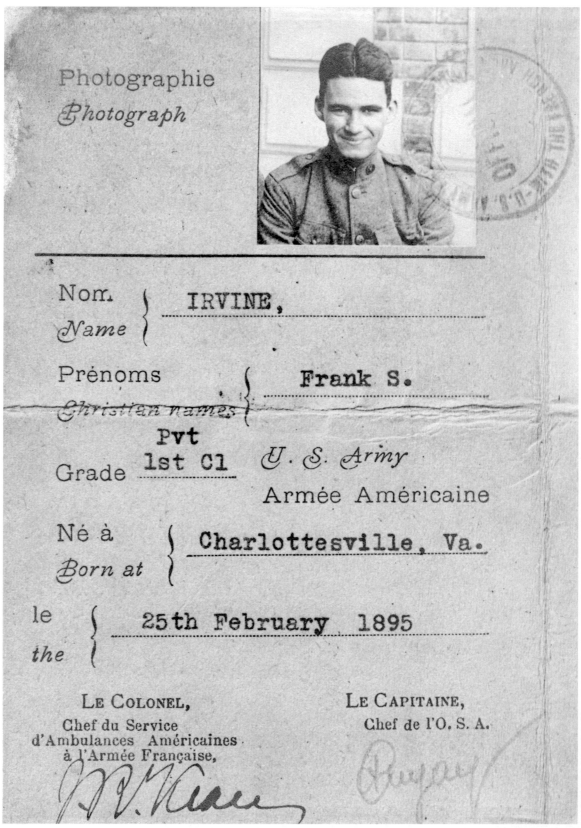

Photographie
Photograph

Nom.
Name } IRVINE,

Prénoms
Christian names } Frank S.

Grade **Pvt 1st Cl** *U. S. Army*
Armée Américaine

Né à
Born at } Charlottesville, Va.

le
the } 25th February 1895

Le Colonel,
Chef du Service
d'Ambulances Américaines
à l'Armée Française,

Le Capitaine,
Chef de l'O. S. A.

Pvt. Franks S. Irvine left the University of Virginia to join Ambulance Unit 517 in France. His promising life was forever altered at the Meuse-Argonne, where he was severely gassed while tending the wounded. An invalid until his early death in 1942, he represented a generation changed forever in the Great War. PRIVATE COLLECTION

CHAPTER 3
DOCTORS, NURSES, DOUGHNUT DOLLIES, AND HELLO GIRLS

Within weeks of the U.S. declaration of war, the Army Nurse Corps shipped teams of nurses to Europe to establish base hospitals before the arrival of the American Expeditionary Forces. As the U.S. moved to send a division to Europe, welfare organizations under the direction of the Red Cross, the Salvation Army, and the Young Men's Christian Association rapidly mobilized as support units. The SS *Red Cross* sent surgeons, nurses, and supplies to the front to expand services and hospitals, and by October 1917, they began their work with the troops.

The Red Cross was the greatest resource for nurses who were trained and equipped for service in the army and navy. The organization also recruited men and taught them first aid procedures before sending them overseas to work as drivers in the Army Ambulance Corps. The Red Cross supported the morale and health of the troops through the establishment of canteens, libraries, live entertainment venues, cinemas, and hospitals.

An important but lesser-known service was providing masks for the many soldiers who survived their wounds but were left with disfiguring injuries. Facial mutilations were horrific: missing noses, mouths, eyes, and jaws, and gaping wounds that required grafts to close. The remaining scars made it impossible for them to function in society or even return to their families. The Red Cross supported Anna Coleman Ladd, who opened a studio that provided facial masks for American and French soldiers. Her mission, through her artistry, was to restore a reasonable quality of life to the men who bore visible and debilitating scars.

The Salvation Army provided religious services, entertainment for the troops, rest and recreation centers, humanitarian aid for prisoners of war, and canteens and tents serving refreshments to soldiers. Doughnuts were a favorite, and the women who served them were affectionately called "doughnut girls" or "doughnut dollies." In a postwar letter, Stella Young described the process of baking the doughnuts near the front lines with few resources: "They made a rolling pin from a wine bottle . . . and they used a baking powder can to cut out the doughnuts and a camphor ice tube to make the hole in the doughnut. They were able to make only a few dozen a day. . . . The poor guys were standing outside, a hundred or two hundred of them in line, smelling the doughnuts frying and waiting for a handful." When the engineers arrived, they made proper rolling pins and doughnut cutters, and the output increased from a few dozen to several thousand per day, vastly improving the comfort and morale of hundreds of battle-weary soldiers.

The Young Men's Christian Association was directed by General Pershing to establish operations near the front to support the morale of the troops. They provided canteens serving coffee and doughnuts, entertainment in tent theaters, recreation huts, personal supplies when available, and assistance with mail services.

The Red Cross, Salvation Army, and YMCA were heavily staffed with volunteers. One of them, Julia Stimson, served as the chief nurse of Base Hospital 21 and was later promoted to the position of director of nursing of the AEF. She expressed her maternal concern for her nursing staff, as their working conditions were difficult, equipment was limited, and working hours were long. She described the nurses as pale, hollow-eyed, and exhausted. With the high number of casualties coming in, everyone was overworked. Their staff quarters provided little comfort from the extreme weather.

Toward the end of 1918, the weary medical staff faced another challenge. An influenza pandemic swept throughout the world, leaving an estimated 50 million dead. More soldiers lost their lives to the flu than to battle injuries, and it was the cause of most of the deaths among the nurses.

The war also brought new challenges to the medical teams, as gas was used as a weapon for the first time. Soldiers exposed to mustard gas suffered burns and damage to their noses, throats, and lungs and often were killed by asphyxiation. Those who survived lingered in pain for the rest of their lives.

Trench warfare forced the troops into dismal conditions. Trenches were often damp or filled with water and infiltrated with rats and lice, providing an ideal environment for the development of diseases such as typhus, pneumonia, and influenza. Trench foot was the result of standing in water-filled trenches for weeks; the only treatment for the most severe cases was amputation. Psychological trauma followed barrages of constant shelling, and the horrors of trench warfare disabled some soldiers with an illness called "shell shock." Those afflicted were unable to function and removed from the lines.

World War I drove the development of innovative medical technology, which doctors brought to the front. They successfully used X-ray equipment to locate bullets and shrapnel during operations and increased survival rates with the introduction of blood transfusions. Improved techniques in the application of antiseptic solutions and clean bandages resulted in a significant reduction in the number of infections.

Dr. John Caldwell, a captain at the Allery Hospital Center during the height of the Meuse-Argonne offensive, wrote to his wife, who was a nurse:

I haven't had time to sit down for four days and I am now stealing a few minutes while a train unloads. In the past week, the hospital trains have come in at all hours pouring patients into our wards. I never knew I could be so tired. I work all day and all night in the ward and the operating rooms and never feel I have finished. I can catch only brief moments of sleep. My only fear is that I have not done enough. That I might have left something undone that makes

for one of my patients comfort or safety. I have four nurses on my ward and how those girls do work. They never seem to tire of lose (*sic*) patients and their attitude is so different from that of civil practice. How I wish you could spend a week here and I know you would itch to be in it and be so proud of our profession.

"Hello Girls" came about in 1917, following General Pershing's request to the War Department for a team of experienced bilingual switchboard operators. (The term was used long before World War I to refer to telephone operators.) These women were sworn in to the Signal Corps and sent to Pershing's headquarters in Chaumont and U.S. Army offices in Paris. The dysfunctional telephone service in France created a serious lapse in effective communication among the American locations. General Pershing waived the language requirement in order to meet the desperate need for efficient service. As the war continued, the operators were assigned to several towns throughout France and England. General Pershing believed women were better suited for switchboard duty, thus relieving the soldiers for combat duty.

"Hello Girls" served as operators at the AEF headquarters at Chaumont and were required to speak both English and French. American servicemen were delighted to speak with them, as they were truly a voice from home. LOC

On Visitor's Day in 1918 at the Naval Training Station, boys take their friends and relatives to the Hostess House at Great Lakes Training Station, Chicago, Illinois. NARA

Cutting hair at the 166th Field Hospital camp, 42nd Division, Baccarat, France, May 15, 1918. NARA

A couple of soldiers enjoy Thanksgiving dinner in 1918 as New York City played host to the boys in service and cared for their men in uniform. NARA

The Jewish Welfare Board hosted its first Passover Seder for men of the Jewish faith in the American Expeditionary Force in Paris, April 1919. NARA

Members of the 101st Field Signal Battalion, 26th Division, at outdoor church services on October 18, 1918, in the ruins of a church destroyed by shell fire in Verdun, France. NARA

A squad of American soldiers listen to one of their comrades playing the organ in the half-wrecked old church in Exermont, in the Argonne, October 11, 1918. NARA

Aix-les-Bains was an AEF rest area with a very popular area known as the Casino, a former restaurant. Here, doughboys sing a song while a few YMCA girls round out the chorus. NARA

Clubs in the States were segregated during the war, so African-American women opened one of their own to care for their men in service. A returning member of the 369th "Harlem Hellfighters," identified by the Croix de Guerre he wears on his shoulder, sits on the couch at right. NARA

Wounded officers and Mrs. Mabelle Corey play bridge on the veranda of Château de Villegenis in Palaiseau, France, on September 18, 1918. Corey was a famous American actress and model and the wife of American steel magnate William Ellis Corey. The Coreys opened their estate in France to wounded American officers. NARA

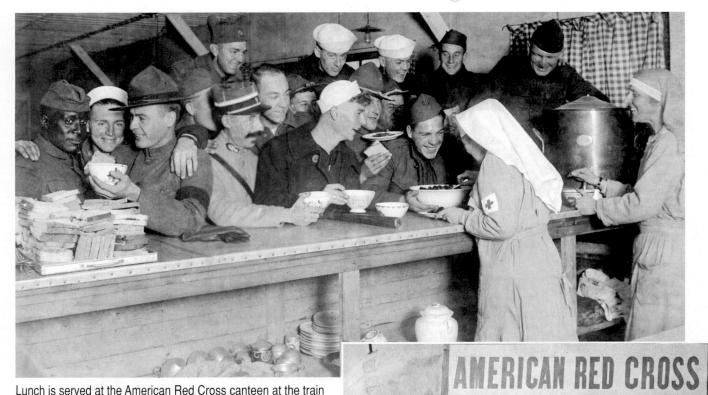

Lunch is served at the American Red Cross canteen at the train station in Bordeaux, France, October 1918. NARA

Time to open the American Red Cross recreation hut at American Military Hospital Number 5 in Auteuil, France, September 1918. NARA

One unit of the famous "Flying Squadron" first-aid service of the American Red Cross in Great Britain prided themselves on being able to get underway within three minutes of the time a call was received. NARA

American Red Cross parade in Birmingham, Alabama, May 21, 1918. NARA

Members of the Medical Corps removing the wounded from Vaux, France, July 22, 1918. NARA

A U.S. Marine receiving first aid before being sent to a hospital in the rear of the trenches, March 22, 1918. NARA

The shattered church in the ruins of Neuvilly furnished a temporary shelter for American wounded being treated by the 110th Sanitary Train, 35th Division, on September 20, 1918. NARA

A Salvation Army worker writes a letter home for a wounded soldier. NARA

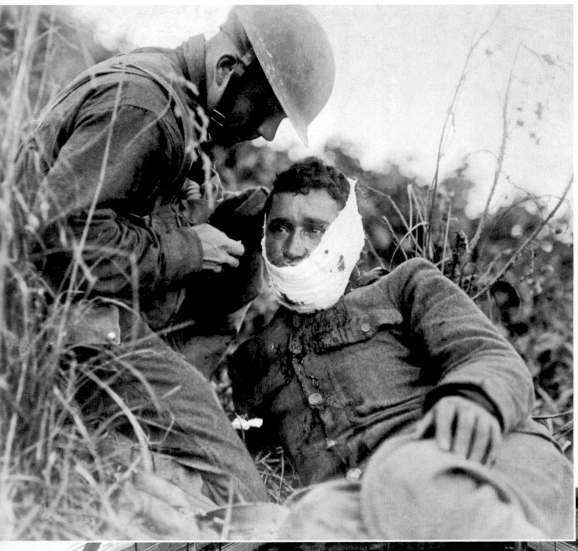

A soldier of Company K, 110th Infantry Regiment, 28th Division, just wounded, receives first aid from a comrade at Varennes-en-Argonne, France, September 26, 1918. NARA

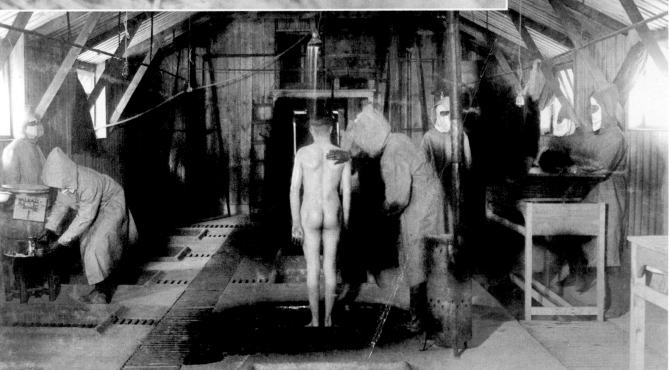

Treatment room for gassed patients in American Evacuation Hospital Number 2, Baccarat, France, June 8, 1918. NARA

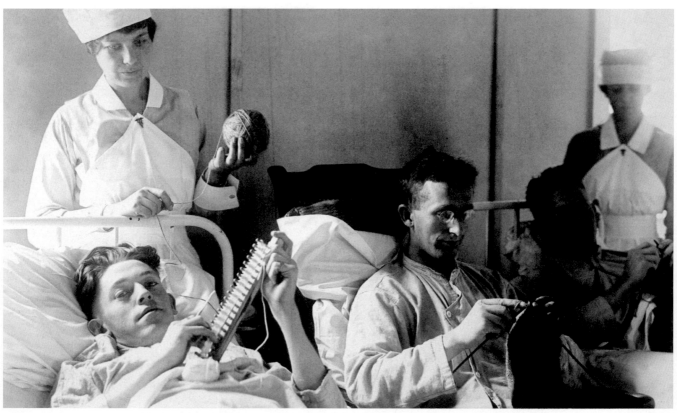

Bedridden wounded knit at Walter Reed Hospital in Washington, D.C., 1918. NARA

Members of the Red Cross host a Christmas dinner for wounded soldiers in 1918. LOC

Director of Nursing Services for the AEF Julia Catherine Stimson sits for an official portrait at the end of the war. LOC

Capt. John Caldwell, an orthopedic surgeon at Base Hospital No. 25, was the son of a U.S. congressman from Ohio. Base Hospital No. 25 was the second to arrive at Allery, France, a large hospital center, and had a capacity of 1,750 beds. The first patients arrived on July 30, 1918, and the highest number of patients in treatment at one time was 1,815 in November 1918. In the course of their assignment, the hospital cared for 2,822 surgical and 3,038 medical cases. PRIVATE COLLECTION

An unidentified member of the Army Nurse Corps (ANC) wears her signature wide-brimmed wool felt hat and blue Norfolk jacket. Note the Army Nurse Corps insignia on her collar featuring the caduceus and "A.N.C." monogram. PRIVATE COLLECTION

Performer Elsie Janis, the "Sweetheart of the AEF," visits the American II Corps at Bruges, France, in July 1918. She is escorted by Col. G. S. Simonds, corps chief of staff, and Gen. Sir Henry Horne, commander of the British First Army. NARA

Although not authorized, this young nurse wears the shoulder sleeve insignia of the District of Paris and a six months' overseas service stripe. PRIVATE COLLECTION

An unidentified army medic sits for a studio portrait proudly sporting his medical arm band. PRIVATE COLLECTION

This postcard depicts soldiers enjoying a moment of relaxation at a Red Cross canteen somewhere in France. PRIVATE COLLECTION

Although this postcard is titled "American wounded after bombardment France," the photo more likely depicts a training exercise in the States. Note the campaign hats, lack of gas masks, and medics exposing themselves to the enemy as two officers casually look on. PRIVATE COLLECTION

This studio portrait of a young captain and doctor assigned to the 89th Division shows the stress of combat. PRIVATE COLLECTION

Pvt. D. L. Greer, Miss H. C. Perry, Pvt. V. Ratman, and Miss P. F. Parkman make doughnuts for the boys of the VII Corps at Dun-sur-Meuse, France, in November 1918. NARA

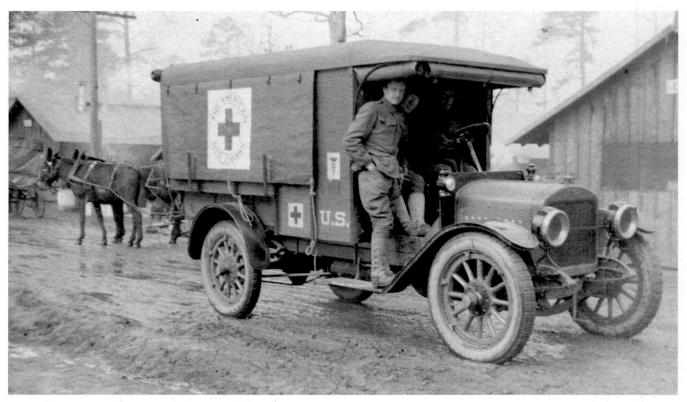

Pvt. Starr A. Miller of the 102nd Field Signal Battalion, 26th Division, poses on an ambulance "Somewhere in France." MHI

American Red Cross workers Adele Birdsall and Miss Thomas provide hot chocolate to a soldier of the 36th Division, Senoncourt, France, October 1918. NARA

With few exceptions, African-American soldiers in the AEF were relegated to labor and support roles. Here, dining car chefs aboard Hospital Train Number 54 in Horreville, France, smile for the photographer on April 26, 1918. NARA

Brig. Gen. Charles G. Treat with American Red Cross nurses in
Villafranca, Italy, July 27, 1918. The AEF sent one regiment, the
332nd Infantry, 83rd Division, to fight on the Italian front. NARA

An unidentified medic stands in front of a barracks building at a
training camp. He wears a belt designed to be filled with
dressings in lieu of ammunition. Each pouch holds two combat
field dressings, along with sublimated gauze and an assortment
of other basic first aid supplies. The large pouch hanging from
the belt holds casualty diagnostic tags. PRIVATE COLLECTION

Stage Women's War Relief. Peggy O'Neil supplied hundreds of American children with yarn and knitting needles to knit garments for soldiers and the destitute children of France and Belgium. NARA

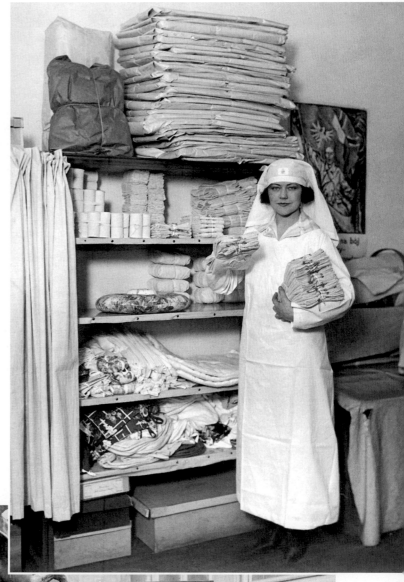

American telephone girls on arrival for "Hello" duty in France. While not formally part of the U.S. Army, "Hello Girls" felt they had earned their place as part of their assigned unit and were thus entitled to wear the insignia, awards, and service devices. Doughboys largely agreed; sadly, the War Department did not. They fought for decades to finally receive the recognition they deserved. NARA

Ambulance crews conducting preparation drills prior to receiving flu victims. LOC

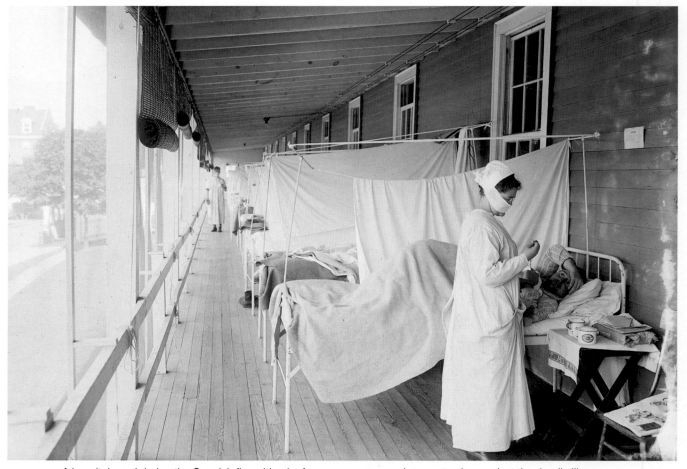

A hospital ward during the Spanish flu epidemic. A nurse wears a mask as protection against the deadly illness. LOC

CHAPTER 4
UNIFORMS, WEAPONS, AND EQUIPMENT

Based on recent combat experience in Cuba and the Philippines, and following the lead of other nations, the U.S. Army transitioned from the traditional "Army Blue" wool uniform to one of khaki or olive-drab at the turn of the twentieth century. By the eve of American involvement in World War I, the Army had adopted a sturdy olive-drab uniform of wool or cotton drill (for use in the tropics). Wool provided durability and historically had proved to retain warmth when wet. The simple, fitted coat featured a five-button front, standing collar with U.S. and branch insignia roundels or collar disks, four patch pockets, and epaulettes. It was very much akin to its British cousin in design, lacking the lavish contrasting trim historically used to denote branch of service or regimental affiliation. Additional insignia initially included only contrasting olive-drab rank, along with simple branch specialty marks, a striking departure from army tradition, which used a designated set of branch colors and devices for rank and specialty insignia. Rank and specialty would be supplemented by mid-war with a system, begrudgingly approved by the War Department, of shoulder sleeve insignia denoting individual soldier corps or division affiliation. Although the army retained the blue uniform for dress occasions, drafted soldiers were not issued the blue dress uniform, by order of the Secretary of War. They wore the khaki field uniform for all occasions.

For colder climes, the soldier was provided with a heavy, below-the-knee, blanket wool overcoat with a double-breasted closure and a button collar. A shorter shawl-collar version of the overcoat was popular with officers, drivers, and laborers.

The accompanying wool shirt and trousers were also of olive-drab. The shirt was a pullover design, half button, with a generous cut in the body and elbows; the trousers were designed like riding breeches, tapering at the calf. The trousers' calves had laces designed to fit the bottom of the trouser tightly to the leg, which in turn was protected with canvas leggings covering the top of the trouser leg and boot, in theory keeping mud, dust, and dirt at bay. The boots were made of rugged, rough-out brown leather designed for marching.

The army retained the long-popular slouch hat, which had come into general use at the end of the Civil War and had only increased in popularity with soldiers during the Western campaigns. The brown wool felt hat's wide brim provided the wearer protection from the sun. The version adopted shortly before the war was dubbed the "Montana Peak" hat, a direct design forebear to today's drill sergeant or "Smokey Bear" hat.

The Department of the Navy retained the traditional blue reefer jacket uniform for officers and chief petty officers, along with the longstanding "Jack Tar" or "Cracker Jack" uniform for enlisted members. Officers and chief petty officers wore a double-breasted navy blue coat with gilt buttons and rank on the shoulder, cuff, or sleeve, respectively. The department underwent a similar transition for its land force, the U.S. Marines, adopting uniforms akin to the army's. These uniforms included a tropical cotton drill khaki tunic, along with a wool uniform in forest green, with standing collar, four pleated pockets, epaulettes, and chevron cuffs. Once the Marines were deployed to France and integrated into the AEF, Pershing prohibited the wear of the forest green uniform and had them issued the standard army coat and pants. Marines continued to wear the Eagle, Globe, and Anchor on their headgear and collar disks, and often switched out the army eagle buttons on the coats to set them apart from their army brethren.

Upon arrival in Europe, the uniform underwent several other important changes. American officers, including Pershing himself, quickly adopted the British Sam Browne belt, a brown leather waist belt with shoulder strap, designed to carry officer field impedimenta. Although rarely used by company grade officers in the trenches, the Sam Browne belt became the symbol, both good and bad, of the officer.

On a more practical level, changes were immediately made to protect soldiers from the daily hazards of life in the trenches. The British Brodie helmet was adopted for combat operations, providing some degree of ballistic protection; while in the garrison environment, the slouch hat was widely discarded in favor of the "overseas cap," a plain, rectangular-shaped, envelope hat, which became the universal sign of overseas men.

The canvas lace-up leggings were jettisoned in favor of the British wool leg wraps, or puttees, which proved far more effective in keeping trench mire out of the boots. Some more fortunate soldiers were able to acquire the British leather jerkin, a wool-lined vest that served as added protection from the elements without the weight of the overcoat. Finally, the boots used in training were replaced with a more robust model, featuring hobnails for traction and steel heel plates and toe caps for better wear.

During the war with Spain and subsequent operations in the Philippines, the army adopted a bolt-action, smokeless powder rifle for the individual soldier. By the eve of the war, the .30-caliber M1903 Springfield was the standard AEF infantryman's weapon; however, production constraints at Springfield Arsenal caused the War Department to issue a second model weapon, the M1917 rifle, to all National Army (draftee) divisions as an emergency measure. Prior to America's entry into the war, a number of factories in the United States were manufacturing the M1917 rifle for British forces. These weapons, produced in .303 caliber, the standard British ammunition size, were quickly retooled into the American .30 caliber for issue to the rapidly expanding armed forces. As such, the AEF deployed with two very different individual infantry rifles.

The standard sidearm of the AEF was the Colt M1911 pistol; this .45-caliber, magazine-fed, semiautomatic weapon saw was widely used by officers and machine gunners and as a supplement to personal protection. Although the Colt M1917 .45-caliber, six-shot revolver was still in general issue and saw extensive use in the AEF, it was far less popular with front-line troops who preferred the M1911's quick-firing stopping power over the double-action revolver.

With very limited exception, American formations relied completely on their Allies for heavy weapons, including machine guns, mortars, and artillery. The French Chauchat Automatic Rifle Model 1915 (machine gun), universally disliked by the American soldiers, and the more popular M1917 British Lewis Automatic Rifle (machine gun) were in wide use by the AEF.

American field artillery employed the British Newton-Stokes mortar and French 75mm and 155mm guns. With the exception of some American Coast Artillery Corps units, who deployed using U.S. Navy guns, all artillery in the AEF was provided by their European allies. Lastly, American tank forces were equipped with the Renault FT-17 light tank, which would play a significant part in AEF operations.

As with the uniform, individual soldier equipage underwent significant changes in the first decade of the twentieth century, with the army transitioning from leather accoutrements to a fully canvas web equipment set. The M1910 equipment featured a ten-pocket cartridge belt that held two five-round clips of .30-06 rifle ammunition in each pocket and could also support a haversack (knapsack), canteen, and individual first aid dressing. The haversack had an integrated meat can pouch, carried the mess tin and eating utensils, and allowed for attachment of a blanket, extra boots, a shovel, and a bayonet. Upon arrival in Europe, soldiers were issued the British (gas mask) Small Box Respirator (SBR) and often, as an emergency backup, the lighter French Mark 2 gas mask.

Overall, the newly minted American army was generally well equipped for the European adventure, with a mixed bag of leadership, training, and weaponry.

Two Coast Artillery soldiers pose in the army dress blue uniform. The army discarded its traditional blue uniform for khaki-colored uniforms based on lessons learned at the turn of the twentieth century. The corporal (seated) wears a gunner insignia. PRIVATE COLLECTION

A young infantryman cuts a bully studio pose with a female companion somewhere out West. He wears the regulation prewar dress uniform, piped with the infantry branch color, and sports a sharpshooter qualification badge on his chest. PRIVATE COLLECTION

This 1919 portrait of a battle-hardened veteran of the 3rd Division stands in sharp contrast to the prewar uniform images. The olive-drab, four-pocket wool uniform is completely utilitarian. He wears the overseas cap and his 3rd Division shoulder sleeve insignia on the left sleeve. The left cuff chevrons identify him as serving eighteen months overseas (six months for each chevron). If the identical chevron was worn in the same position on the right sleeve, it indicated wounds (one for each chevron). Finally, he wears a Victory Ribbon and marksmanship medal. PRIVATE COLLECTION

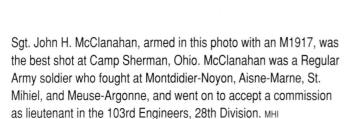

Sgt. John H. McClanahan, armed in this photo with an M1917, was the best shot at Camp Sherman, Ohio. McClanahan was a Regular Army soldier who fought at Montdidier-Noyon, Aisne-Marne, St. Mihiel, and Meuse-Argonne, and went on to accept a commission as lieutenant in the 103rd Engineers, 28th Division. MHI

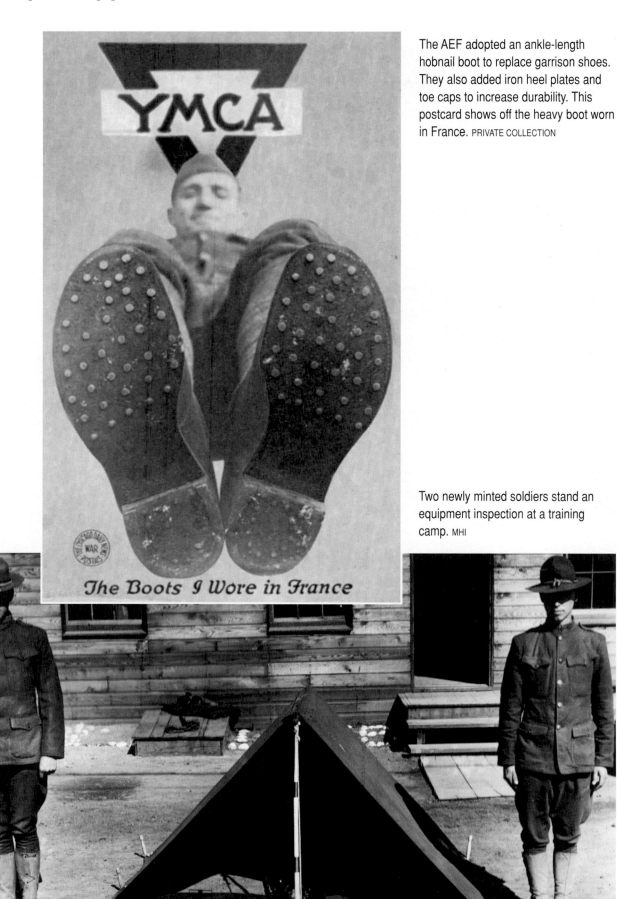

The AEF adopted an ankle-length hobnail boot to replace garrison shoes. They also added iron heel plates and toe caps to increase durability. This postcard shows off the heavy boot worn in France. PRIVATE COLLECTION

Two newly minted soldiers stand an equipment inspection at a training camp. MHI

The Boots I Wore in France

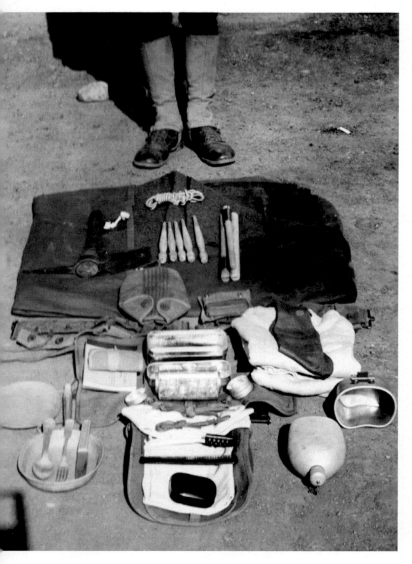

A closer view of the equipment laid out for inspection, showing the mess kit, canteen, and open haversack. MHI

This comic postcard mocks a soldier's load but plainly shows the arrangement of a correctly packed haversack/knapsack. The blanket is packed inside the haversack; the overcoat is rolled in a horseshoe, while a shovel, extra boots, and helmet hang over the meat tin pouch containing the mess kit. PRIVATE COLLECTION

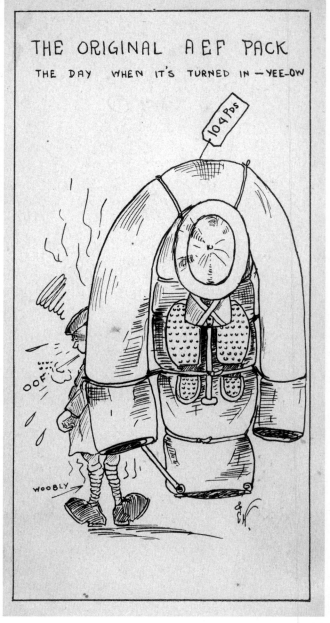

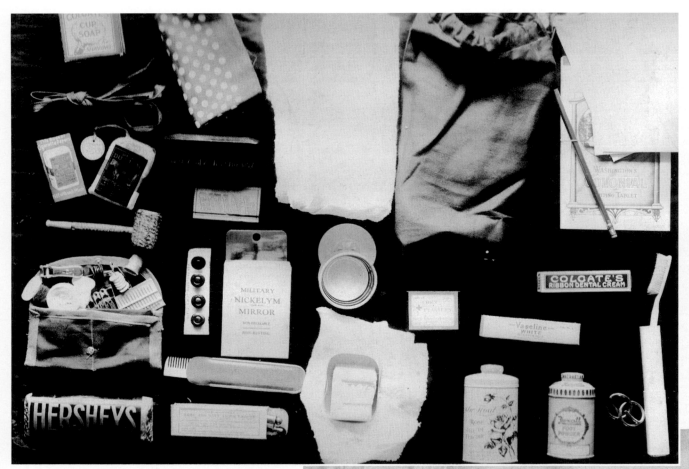

When available, Komfort Kits were issued to each soldier, containing a variety of items to make life in the army bearable. MHI

This photo, taken "Right Before the Armistice 1918," shows members of Battery D, 311th Field Artillery, 79th Division. Helmets replace campaign hats and puttees replace leggings on these combat soldiers. PRIVATE COLLECTION

Although taken after the Armistice, this postcard illustrates the uniform prevalent in the AEF. The reverse reads, "A real view of a [sic] AEF Soldier— with field shoes and heavy clothing. My clothes ain't pressed very much this day and no shoes to shine. This is all I have on New Year's Day so you can see how cold it is here." PRIVATE COLLECTION

Four soldiers, identified as Privates Harry Bergoffer, Arthur Ourig, Emil Meyer, and Bert Seifert, stand guard in Boucq, France, in April 1919. They wear the standard army wool overcoat and carry M-1917 rifles. PRIVATE COLLECTION

Illustrating the wartime uniforms of the navy and the army, a navy petty officer, second class (signalman), stands next to his brother, a soldier in the 1st Division wearing four overseas service chevrons. PRIVATE COLLECTION

This young Marine, probably assigned to the Marine Barracks, Washington, D.C., wears the regulation forest green Marine Corps uniform of World War I. Pershing specifically forbade wearing this uniform overseas. Marines overseas wore the army uniform. PRIVATE COLLECTION

This proud member of the 372nd Infantry Regiment, as indicated by the "Bloody Hand" shoulder sleeve insignia, wears two Croix de Guerre on his chest. PRIVATE COLLECTION

The 369th Infantry Regiment "Harlem Hellfighters," or "Rattlers," often wore a rattlesnake shoulder sleeve insignia, as pictured. This soldier's decorations include the Croix de Guerre, as indicated by the lanyard. PRIVATE COLLECTION

Pvt. Oliver Boron, Headquarters Company, 66th Field Artillery, stands in front of a French farm building. He wears a pistol belt with a half-moon clip pouch for an M1917 Colt revolver. PRIVATE COLLECTION

The army also issued a denim fatigue uniform for labor, as worn by this soldier. PRIVATE COLLECTION

H. J. Boland of the 78th Division wears his small box respirator and helmet for a patriotic studio photo. PRIVATE COLLECTION

A group of officers from the 108th Field Artillery Regiment, 28th Division, pose with Maj. Harold Hellyer. They wear the typical attire of officers in the AEF, including Sam Browne belt and boots. PRIVATE COLLECTION

Cpl. Clifford C. Catlin, Company B, 31st Infantry Regiment, wears the "Shackleton gear" issued to the Siberian AEF in this Russian photo. The AEF sent three regiments to Russia—the 27th, 31st, and 339th Infantry—along with attachments. PRIVATE COLLECTION

The 81st Division is generally credited with the creation of shoulder sleeve divisional patches in the AEF. According to the December 1919 National Geographic magazine:

> In the summer of 1918 the War Department received a communication from the commanding general, Port of Embarkation, Hoboken, reporting that all members of the Eighty-first Division, at that time going through the port on their way to France, were wearing a "wildcat" in cloth on the arm, and requesting information regarding the authority for this device. . . . On arrival of this division in France difficulties were at once encountered. The existence of the device was reported to General Headquarters and the Commanding General [Maj. Gen. Charles J. Bailey] was directed to remove the insignia. He protested, saying that by its silence the War Department had tacitly authorized it; that it was most desirable, in order that the officers might readily know the men of the division; and, finally, that it was highly prized by the personnel and therefore was a great help toward maintaining and improving the morale of the command. It so happened that General Headquarters had been studying the question of identification of units in battle. Experience had shown that some method was necessary for quickly reassembling troops after an offensive. Organizations became confused, and after an advance they are almost inextricably mixed. To reassemble under their own officers rapidly is an important point. . . . The "wildcat" of the Eighty-first Division seemed to offer a solution of the problem, and as a result it was authorized and the commanding generals of all combat divisions in France were at once directed to select insignia for their divisions.

This patch is the standard variety that the division selected—a black silhouette of a wildcat on a khaki circle. Several variations exist where the color of the wildcat varies according to the different arms of the service: for example, a white cat and khaki surround for the 161st Infantry Brigade, a white cat and orange surround or blue cat and khaki surround for the 162nd Infantry Brigade, a red cat with khaki surround for artillery/ammunition train, a buff cat with khaki surround for the 306th Supply Train, a yellow cat with blue surround for the 306th Signal Battalion, and a green cat with khaki surround for the 306th Sanitary Train. PRIVATE COLLECTION

Two 332nd Infantry Regiment, 84th Division, soldiers in full marching order show the M1910 equipment set. The 332nd Infantry Regiment was the one unit in the AEF that served on the Italian front. LOC

An unknown African-American soldier poses wearing a popular variation of the army overcoat, the mackinaw. This shorter version featured a shawl collar. MHI

A portrait of an unidentified 92nd Division soldier wearing the division shoulder sleeve insignia and a pistol qualification badge. MHI

Army field clerk Will Judy, of the headquarters, U.S. 33rd Division, remarked presciently in his journal, "The airplane gets half our entire attention. It goes everywhere; it brings destruction; it moves quickly; it is a great spy; it does the work of a thousand rifles; it scares us; it makes us helpless against its dropping death; it seems to be most of the war."

A technology barely two decades old, powered flight evolved significantly during the course of the war. The airplane and its combat formations quickly took on expanding roles far beyond the air-to-air dogfights that became a Great War cliché. The airplane undertook a wide array of missions, including artillery observation, reconnaissance, air-to-ground attack, and bombing, including medium- and long-range missions.

The air war created its own host of heroes, many of whom became household names, including Germany's first ace and *Pour le Mérite* winner Lt. Max Immelman; Baron (Major) Manfred von Richthofen, the commanding officer of the Flying Circus and the war's highest scoring ace, credited with eighty victories; and Germany's highest-scoring ace to survive the war, Lt. Ernst Udet, with sixty-two kills.

The Allies had their own share of champions, including French fighter pilot Capt. René Fonck, with seventy-five victories; French daredevil Capt. Georges Guynemer with fifty-four victories; and British aces Maj. Edward Mannock with seventy-three combat credits, Lt. Col. William A. Bishop with seventy-two kills, and Capt. Albert Ball, recipient of the Victoria Cross and credited with forty-four victories. American aces included Capt. Eddie Rickenbacker with twenty-six air conquests, and "Balloon Buster" Lt. Frank Luke, Jr., with eighteen kills.

By the Armistice, air power had proven to be a vital element of future warfare. Civilian and military leaders marveled at the potential demonstrated during the crude bombings of London and Paris, experiments with parachutes, and the aircraft's prospects as a combat multiplier.

Maj. William Lacey Kenly (right, in basket), chief of the Air Service and director of Military Aeronautics, prepares to go aloft in a balloon. Kenly, soon to be promoted to brigadier general, is considered by many to be the father of the Army Air Corps and the U.S. Air Force. LOC

Perhaps the most famous fighter ace of all time, and certainly the one of greatest renown from World War I, *Freiherr Rittmeister* (Baron Captain) Manfred von Richthofen, is linked in American popular culture to the war—thanks to his air battles with Snoopy. Richthofen perfected air combat and is credited with eighty combat victories. LOC

Twenty-six airplanes in line for inspection at the aviation field at Issoudon, France, in April 1918. NARA

The 148th Aero Squadron was a pursuit squadron assigned to the Royal Air Force and took part in British operations until it was reassigned to U.S. Second Army on November 4, 1918. This squadron accomplished numerous patrols over enemy lines, fought 107 air combat missions, and received confirmation for 71 victories. In this photo, squadron members are making preparations for a daylight raid on German trenches and cities, with their aircraft lined up and the pilots and mechanics testing the planes prior to takeoff on August 6, 1918. NARA

First Lt. Eddie Rickenbacker, 94th Aero Squadron—the "Hat in the Ring" squadron—standing up in his SPAD plane near Rembercourt, France, on October 18, 1918. Perhaps one of the most famous members of the AEF, Rickenbacker was a recipient of the Medal of Honor and America's top fighter pilot, with twenty-six aerial victories. Postwar, Rickenbacker was a famous racecar driver and a noted pioneer in civil aviation. His contributions as chairman of Eastern Air Lines have had a lasting impact on commercial aviation into the present century. NARA

Official portrait of Capt. Edward Rickenbacker, 1919.
NARA

The insignia of the 94th Aero Squadron, known as the "Hat in the Ring" squadron. World War I saw the birth of painted squadron insignia on aircraft. Unlike the racy insignia of their World War II offspring, most squadron insignia of the Great War featured "G-rated" patriotic themes. The 94th Aero Squadron engaged in operations in the Toul Sector, at Château-Thierry, at St. Mihiel, and in the Meuse-Argonne first and second offensives. The squadron accomplished 304 patrols, fought 114 combats, and is credited with 64 kills. The name alludes to America's entry into the war—when we threw our hat in the ring. DAUGHTERS OF THE AMERICAN LEGION MAGAZINE

Second Lt. Lawrence S. Churchill at Rockwell Field, San Diego, California, 1915. Churchill would rise to command the 4th Composite Group, Far East Air Force, in the Philippines before World War II and spent time in a Japanese prisoner-of-war camp, retiring in 1947 after a long career. NARA

Lt. Earl Carroll, an aviator in the U.S. Air Service, poses beside his fast scout plane. Carroll was a prominent composer and Broadway playwright before the war and the very stereotype of the daredevil combat pilot. Postwar, Carroll parlayed his reputation as a bad boy, gaining the title "the Troubadour of the Nude," by staging productions featuring the most risqué showgirls in New York. In 1926, Carroll was embroiled in a scandal when, at one of his parties, a nude woman was brought out in a bathtub filled with illegal liquor; the stunt ended with a six-month prison sentence. Carroll continued his writing career until his ironic death in a commercial airplane crash in 1948. NARA

An unidentified pilot from the 91st Aero Squadron, an army observation squadron. The 91st was assigned to I Corps and was engaged in operations in the Toul Sector and at St. Mihiel and the Meuse-Argonne. The squadron flew 104 air combat missions and brought down 21 German planes. Note the squadron insignia on the aircraft, consisting of a mounted knight in pursuit of a winged devil whose blood he has already drawn with the lance. NARA

First Lt. Joseph M. Carberry stands in front of a Curtiss Model G at Rockwell Field, San Diego, California, in 1914. Carberry, a West Point graduate, was one of the early pioneers of aviation, becoming one of the first qualified army aviators. He served as an observer during the operations along the Mexican border and remained in service throughout the war. NARA

First Air Depot repairs damaged planes in Colomby, France. NARA

"Balloon Buster" Lt. Frank Luke, Jr., after he brought down three German observation balloons in thirty-five minutes. He was the first airman to receive the Medal of Honor and the second-ranking American ace, credited with eighteen victories, topped only by Rickenbacker. On September 29, 1918, Luke was mortally wounded while on a mission during the Meuse-Argonne offensive and perished shortly after landing his plane behind enemy lines. NARA

The German plane C.L III A 3892/18, brought down in the Argonne on October 4, 1918, by American machine gunners between Montfaucon and Cierges, France, shows the Iron Cross painted on the wings and fuselage of enemy planes. NARA

A German aviator drops a bomb somewhere on the Western Front. Soldiers found bombs from aircraft particularly unnerving, as their deadly reach into quiet sectors seemed both limitless and wholly arbitrary. NARA

An Aeroplane Graflex camera in action. Despite our current notions of widespread dogfighting along the Western Front, commanders predominantly used airplanes for observation, artillery spotting, and intelligence. Photographs of troop concentrations and trench fortifications and positions were especially valued. NARA

Capt. A. W. Stevens (center, front row) and personnel of the14th Photo Section, First Army, "The Balloonatic Section." NARA

A balloon ascending at Camp de Meucon. Each balloon company consisted of single balloon. NARA

A close-up view of an American major in the basket of an observation balloon flying over territory near the front lines in June 1918. NARA

President Woodrow Wilson addresses a joint session of Congress. After much reflection, Wilson felt he was compelled to ask for a declaration of war on Germany on April 2, 1917. LOC

Young soldiers cheer and beckon others to join them as they depart for France. PRIVATE COLLECTION

This song sheet imparts the promise made by so many departing doughboys: "I'll come back home to you when the war is over." PRIVATE COLLECTION

This comic card speaks to the average soldier's best memory in training camp. PRIVATE COLLECTION

This song sheet conveys public euphoria surrounding the Franco-American alliance. The most prevalent theme at the time focused on America's repaying the debt to France for her assistance during the American Revolution. Figures representing Gen. John J. Pershing and Marshall Ferdinand Foch shake hands across the Atlantic as the nation mobilizes. PRIVATE COLLECTION

Sheet music expressed popular opinion. Many Americans believed America had ignored the plight of civilized Europe in her struggle against Germany. When war was declared, much of the population agreed that America had finally awoken. PRIVATE COLLECTION

The James Montgomery Flagg "I Want You" poster. CMH

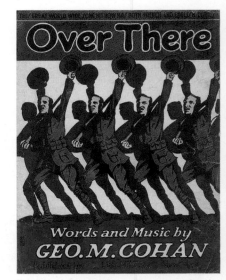

The title of the most famous song associated with the American experience in World War I proudly announces the arrival of the doughboys overseas. PRIVATE COLLECTION

American Expeditionary Force members left the United States with the promise that they would "Bring home the Bacon." PRIVATE COLLECTION

By the time America entered the war, the German infantryman had evolved into a battle-hardened, highly efficient killer. This German poster shows a stormtrooper in a trench, holding a grenade. The text reads, "And you? Subscribe to the 7th War Loan." LOC

The issue of the J. Paul Verrees "Join the Air Service" poster resulted in the most enlistments of any period of the war. LOC

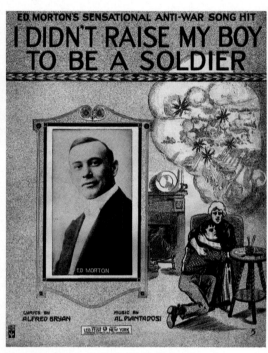

Not everyone was thrilled with the declaration of war on the Central Powers and the alliance with the French and British. Significant numbers of German-Americans, Irish-Americans, and some recent immigrants—particularly those from Austria-Hungary's empire—opposed the war. PRIVATE COLLECTION

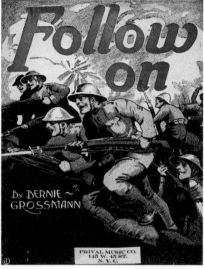

The song sheet "Follow On" imagines a heroic charge across no-man's-land. PRIVATE COLLECTION

A doughboy with sleeves rolled up and ready to complete his work declares that he wants a "Piece of the Rhine." PRIVATE COLLECTION

As her dog looks on, a Dutch child presents a token of her thanks to a ragged doughboy proudly carrying a captured German helmet as a symbol of victory. PRIVATE COLLECTION

The French made much of the importance of Joan of Arc, particularly focusing on the Cathedral at Reims, where Joan performed one of her miracles. "Pershing's Crusaders" plays on the somewhat ironic connection between the American army and Joan of Arc: In the case of the Maid Joan, she fought to free France from the yoke of the English. PRIVATE COLLECTION

On the Trail of the Hun, St. Mihiel Drive by William James Aylward. CMH

Sunday Morning At Cunel by Harvey Thomas Dunn. CMH

Battle Scene with Barbed Wire by Samuel Johnson Woolf. Woolf spent four months with the AEF as an artist for *Collier's Weekly*; shortly after his return to New York, he produced a series of oil paintings conveying his experiences. CMH

Battle Scene by Samuel Johnson Woolf. CMH

Carry On by Samuel Johnson Woolf. CMH

The Intelligence Section by Samuel Johnson Woolf. German prisoners stand before an intelligence officer as a French liaison officer looks on. CMH

Soldier Smoking Samuel Johnson Woolf. A battle-fatigued member of the AEF decompresses in this evocative portrait. CMH

Soldiers in a Bombed Out Town by Samuel Johnson Woolf. A soldier drinks coffee on a break on the march forward. CMH

Military Procession at Mailly le Camp by Samuel Johnson Woolf. CMH

C. Clarke, bugler, 15th New
York Infantry [later the 369th
Infantry Regiment, 93rd
Division], Champagne, France,
by Raymond Desvarreux. CMH

First Aid Station at Seicheprey
by Samuel Johnson Woolf.
CMH

A Night March by Samuel Johnson
Woolf. An army unit slogs on through
a rainstorm, moving to the front. CMH

The standard army tunic of the AEF. As indicated by the shoulder sleeve insignia, this example belongs to a member of M Company from one of the four infantry regiments of the 26th Division. The service chevrons designate eighteen months overseas; the red chevron designates that the soldier was honorably discharged, worn to fend off overzealous military policemen and entitling the veteran to free train transportation. MILITARY AND HISTORICAL IMAGE BANK

A tunic attributed to the Supply Company, the 6th Marine Regiment, 2nd Division, identifiable by the shoulder sleeve insignia. The star, with Indian head insignia, indicates the 2nd Division, the diamond shape designates the 6th Marine Regiment, and the green coloring denotes the Supply Company. This is an example of the standard-issue Marine Corps uniform of the wartime period. Generally, these uniforms were not worn in theater by the AEF, having been forbidden as part of Pershing's effort to maintain a homogenous land force. MILITARY AND HISTORICAL IMAGE BANK

The billed cap of an officer. This type of cap was first adopted at the turn of the century, and its use continued throughout the war. Officer caps were distinguished by the mohair braid and eagle insignia. MILITARY AND HISTORICAL IMAGE BANK

"Hello Girls," the telephone operators at the AEF headquarters, were issued a unique uniform. This unusual example includes the shoulder sleeve insignia for the Versailles Peace Talks delegation, along with an operator qualification device, a Toll Operator brassard, and a six months overseas service chevron. MILITARY AND HISTORICAL IMAGE BANK

A closer view of the collar of an enlisted uniform, showing the collar disc insignia. Components were indicated on the right side by either "U.S." for the Regular Army, "U.S.N.G." for the National Guard, or "U.S.N.A." for the National Army (draftee divisions). The left side specified branch and, in many cases, unit—in this example, the 332nd Infantry Regiment, Company I. Officers wore both component (Regular Army, National Guard, or National Army) and branch insignia on their collars. MHI

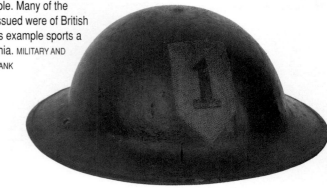

The War Department chose to adopt the British Brodie helmet; shown here is a typical example. Many of the helmets initially issued were of British manufacture. This example sports a 1st Division insignia. MILITARY AND HISTORICAL IMAGE BANK

The "Montana Peak" campaign hat, typically worn in training in the United States. The helmet would replace the campaign hat in combat, while the overseas cap became the preferred headgear away from the front. The army wore the campaign hat with branch-colored hat cords, while the Marines wore the Eagle, Globe, and Anchor device in its place. This example belonged to Pvt. Felix Apple of the Headquarters, 5th Marine Regiment, who inscribed his battle honors on the brim. MILITARY AND HISTORICAL IMAGE BANK

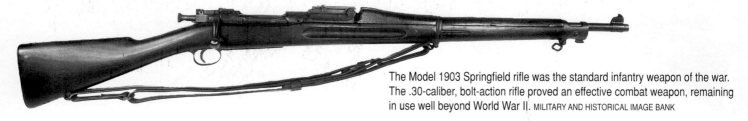

The Model 1903 Springfield rifle was the standard infantry weapon of the war. The .30-caliber, bolt-action rifle proved an effective combat weapon, remaining in use well beyond World War II. MILITARY AND HISTORICAL IMAGE BANK

With the rapidly expanding military, the Springfield Armory could not meet demand for its weapons. The M1917 rifle, manufactured by several American companies under contract for the British army, was adopted as an emergency measure for National Army units. This photo shows a comparison of the two weapons: the M1903 Springfield (bottom) and the M1917 (top). MHI

This close-up of the two bolt-action assemblies (M1917 at top, M1903 at bottom) further illustrates the differences between the two rifles. Though the M1917 was reliable, its awkward action made it unpopular with soldiers. MHI

The .45-caliber M1911 automatic pistol was the standard sidearm of the AEF. The hard-hitting, robust 1911 remained in use in the military forces into the mid-1980s. MILITARY AND HISTORICAL IMAGE BANK

Revolvers saw use as secondary weapons in the AEF, and a number of types were used. This M1917 revolver is a typical example, serving as an apt personal protection weapon. MILITARY AND HISTORICAL IMAGE BANK

The Fusil Mitrailleur Modele 1915 CSRG, or French Chauchat automatic rifle, was the light machine gun widely issued to AEF units. Universally unpopular, many of the weapon's features, including the open magazine designed to indicate remaining ammunition, proved unworthy for trench warfare. MILITARY AND HISTORICAL IMAGE BANK

The army adopted a trench shotgun for close combat, despite objections that it violated the rules of war. The M1898 Winchester trench shotgun saw some service at the front. MILITARY AND HISTORICAL IMAGE BANK

The French 75mm gun of Battery C, 6th Field Artillery Regiment, 1st Division, that fired the first American shot of the war. The gun was brought back and displayed as part of the Liberty Loan drives and is now on exhibit at the West Point Museum, West Point, New York. CMH

This montage illustrates the great variety of shoulder sleeve insignia designs that sprang up once the AEF headquarters began requesting approval of distinctive unit insignia. These patterns represent the Regular Army (top left), National Guard (top right), and National Army (bottom). PRIVATE COLLECTION

An Advance Section, Service of Supply, insignia similar to the one worn in the top photo on page 176. The patch features the Cross of Lorraine, the area where American forces were assigned, and the letters "A" and "S" for Advanced Section. PRIVATE COLLECTION

Members of the Army of Occupation largely wore this insignia. Given the Armistice and the army's principal mission of the occupation of Germany, the insignia was a monogram for Army of Occupation. PRIVATE COLLECTION

This rare example from the War Department files has the notation, "Emblem of the 2nd Division, Regular, AEF. Designed by Sergeant L. D. Lundey, Co A Supply Train. Passed on and approved by Major General Bundy and staff in the month of April, 1918." A series of shapes, including a shield, rectangle, square, and diamond, was used to identify subordinate unit insignia within the 2nd Division. The color of the shape further delineated the unit: headquarters was black; 1st battalion, red; 2nd battalion, yellow; 3rd battalion, blue; machine-gun company, purple; and supply company, green. MHI

This poster, designed to attract African-American recruits, shows President Lincoln watching proudly as African-American soldiers drive back the German enemy. MHI

A German propaganda poster announces that the U-boats are out. PRIVATE COLLECTION

In this illustration, a soldier's pretty sweetheart shows off her beau's Distinguished Service Cross for valor. PRIVATE COLLECTION

Members of the AEF fondly remembered the ladies at the Salvation Army huts who provided a place to escape the ever-present military culture. PRIVATE COLLECTION

Ready to return to the States, a veteran infantryman holds his Bible in this striking image. MHI

Artist Alonzo Earl Foringer captured the essence of the American Red Cross in this iconic poster. CMH

A recruiting poster asks men to join the navy. LOC

On the back of this card, 3rd Division soldier George Arnold wrote his father, "Well we spent the 4th on the Rhine this year but I think it will be the last one we will ever celebrate in Germany. Hope to be home about August 1st." PRIVATE COLLECTION

A colorful French postcard celebrates the success of the Franco-American alliance. PRIVATE COLLECTION

This postcard depicting the "Gibraltar of the Rhine" carries a similar message: We will be homeward bound soon! PRIVATE COLLECTION

The dapper doughboy arrives to an audience of swooning admirers; sadly, the future was bleak for many veterans, who found returning to civilian life challenging. PRIVATE COLLECTION

Stella May Young became the face of the "Doughnut Dolly" after a Signal Corps photographer snapped a picture of her serving doughnuts in the Toul sector in 1918. This sheet music image was directly copied from that photo. Stella gave her life to the Salvation Army, serving overseas again during World War II. She died still actively involved in charity work just short of her ninety-third birthday. PRIVATE COLLECTION

This song sheet pays tribute to "My Red Cross Girlie." Many a soldier fell in love with the ladies who nursed them back to health. PRIVATE COLLECTION

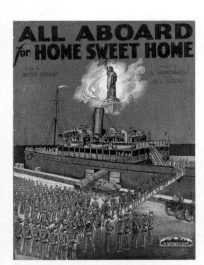

Just as they did following the declaration of war, Tin Pan Alley mobilized for the return of the victorious AEF. This song sheet celebrates the day every doughboy waited for: loading up for the trip home. PRIVATE COLLECTION

An American eagle swoops down to attack a U-boat on this song sheet. LOC

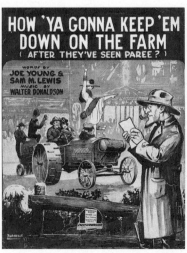

Many a parent wondered if the war, and then the occupation, would change their sons and daughters. This song expressed that concern. PRIVATE COLLECTION

A Trench Ambulance on the Firing Line by Samuel Johnson Woolf.
CMH

Traffic to Mont St. Père, by George Matthews Harding, illustrates the routine congestion prevailing on small French roads during operations. CMH

Two assistant gunners move ammunition boxes while a determined gunner engages the enemy. *A Machine Gun Nest*, Samuel Johnson Woolf. CMH

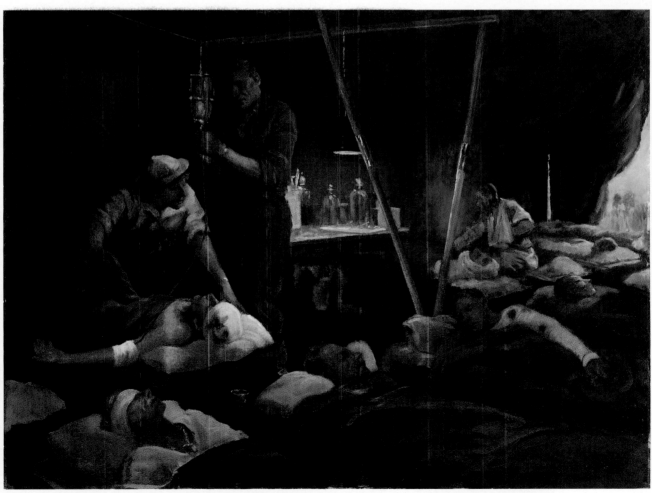

An Army nurse comforts her patient in a crowded ward in this Samuel Johnson Woolf painting entitled *Hospital Scene*. CMH

Crucifix and Dead Soldier,
Samuel Johnson Woolf. CMH

Soldiers at Camp
depicts two Doughboy
guards marching a
group of German
prisoners to their
temporary home in a
prisoner-of-war cage,
Samuel Johnson
Woolf. CMH

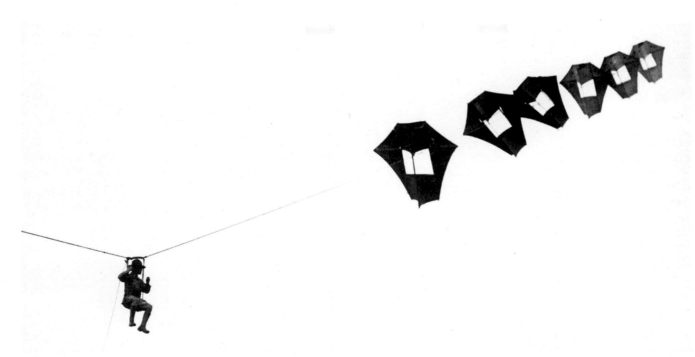

Lt. Kirk Booth of the U.S. Signal Corps is lifted skyward by the giant Perkins man-carrying kite at Camp Devens, Massachusetts. The army conducted extensive testing, seeking new methods of air observation. NARA

An aerial naval observer comes down from a "blimp"-type balloon after a U-boat scouting tour somewhere on the Atlantic Coast. NARA

Second Lt. W. Brown of the 1st Aero Squadron crash-landed his plane in Commune de la Saints, France, on July 6, 1918, after an observation flight over German lines,. Note the squadron insignia prominently displayed on the side of the fuselage. The 1st Aero Squadron was organized and operated as a Corps Observation squadron. It was assigned to the I Corps on April 8, 1918, and was engaged in operations in the Toul Sector, Château-Thierry, St. Mihiel, and the Meuse-Argonne first and second offensives; after the Armistice, it was assigned to the Army of Occupation. This squadron suffered twenty-six casualties, consisting of fifteen killed, eight wounded, two prisoners, and one missing. It engaged in ninety-four combats and was officially credited with shooting down thirteen enemy aircraft. The 1st Aero Squadron was a continuation of the 1st Squadron in the United States Air Service, which began its service on the Mexican border. NARA

Capt. W. C. Schauffler, Jr. (standing), and Lt. Fred A. Tillman of the 90th Aero Squadron stand by their plane prior to a mission at Béthelainville, France, November 18, 1918. The 90th Aero Squadron was a Corps Observation squadron. The squadron insignia depicts a pair of dice with the "lucky" number seven uppermost. The squadron was assigned to the III Corps Observation Group and took part in the operations in the Toul Sector, in St. Mihiel, and in the Meuse-Argonne first and second offensives. This squadron carried out numerous reconnaissance missions, fought twenty-three combats, and received official confirmation for seven victories. It suffered three casualties, consisting of two killed and one wounded. It was demobilized on December 19, 1918. NARA

A French Breguet bomber of the 96th Aero Squadron, piloted by 1st Lt. A. B. Alexander, with 2nd Lt. E. McLennon as observer, prepares to take off from Amanty Field, Amanty, France, July 29, 1918. The squadron insignia is a red devil preparing to launch an aerial bomb; the figure is placed on a white triangular background. NARA

An aerial observation camera is handed to Lt. J. H. Snyder of the 91st Aero Squadron before a reconnaissance mission from Gondreville-sur-Moselle in August, 1918. The pilot is Maj. J. N. Reynolds. NARA

The basket of a captive observation balloon at Brouville, France, April 1918, prior to launch; of particular note are the telephone speaker and headphones worn by the observer and the large map board suspended on the side of the basket. NARA

An observation balloon is reeled in at Camp de Souge, France, April 1918, after a spotting mission. NARA

Lt. Field E. Kindley of the 148th Aero Squadron with his mascot, Fokker, an English Bull Terrier, ready for a flight over German lines. Remaisnil, Somme, France, September 9, 1918. The 148th Aero Squadron was a pursuit squadron assigned to the 4th Pursuit Group, Second Army, on November 4, 1918. This squadron had previously been assigned with the Royal Air Force on July 20, 1918, and had taken part in British operations up until it was assigned to the Second Army. The squadron accomplished many patrols over the enemy lines, fought 107 combats, and received official confirmation for 71 victories. It suffered eleven casualties, consisting of three killed, three wounded, four taken prisoner, and one missing. NARA

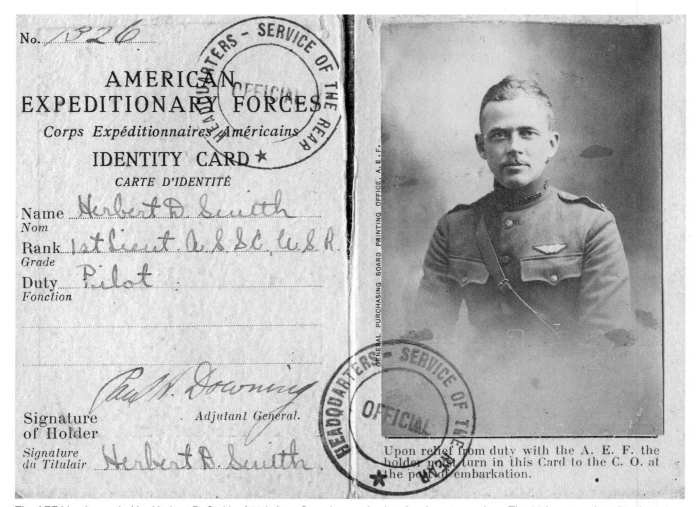

The AEF identity card of Lt. Herbert D. Smith of 96th Aero Squadron, a day bombardment squadron. The 96th was assigned to the 1st Day Bombardment Group, First Army, on May 29, 1918, and was engaged in the operations in the Toul Sector, at St. Mihiel, and in the Meuse-Argonne first and second offensives. This squadron made multiple bombing raids into Germany, destroying a significant amount of enemy property and gathering much valuable information. It fought nineteen combats and was officially credited with downing fourteen enemy airplanes. The squadron suffered forty-one casualties, consisting of twelve killed, twelve wounded, fifteen taken prisoner, and two missing. It ceased operations December 11, 1918. Lieutenant Smith was present at the squadron's most unfortunate event. On July 10, 1918, while stationed at Amanty, the squadron commander, Maj. Harry Brown, took six of his French Breguet bombers out on a mission in particularly poor weather. Quickly becoming disoriented due to low clouds and with their planes running out of fuel, the pilots were forced to land behind German lines. The enemy captured all of the aircraft intact and twelve crewmembers, including Smith. The following day, the Germans dropped a note at a nearby American airfield reading, "Thank you for the fine planes and equipment, but what shall we do with the Major?" Smith survived his POW experience and was returned to American control following the Armistice. PRIVATE COLLECTION

Adorned with sunglasses and sporting the flyboy look, an unidentified first lieutenant leans against an army staff car adorned with an Air Service roundel, the standard marking on AEF aircraft. PRIVATE COLLECTION

Lt. G. R. Melvin, serving with the Air Service Esquadrille #3, Group 12 (French), 1st Division, at Cœuvres-et-Valsery, France, on July 16, 1918. Melvin wears French pilot wings on the right side of his chest and American wings on the left. NARA

An American balloon clearly showing the Allied Air Service roundel. NARA

Capt. Fiorello LaGuardia, future New York City mayor, flew Italian Caproni bombers for the AEF Air Service on the Italian front. LOC

Brig. Gen. William "Billy" Mitchell commanded all American combat air units by the end of the war. During the postwar period, he became an outspoken advocate for airpower. Here, dressed in civilian clothes, he smiles at a press photographer despite his growing troubles with the War Department. LOC

A soldier from the 173rd Aero Squadron drums in the Armistice. The painting on the drum is a caricature of Kaiser Wilhelm II, the symbol of the Allies' "beaten" enemy. MHI

Secretary of the Treasury William J. McAdoo and his son, William, Jr., who was serving in the aviation branch of the navy. The younger McAdoo wears the navy green aviation tunic with ensign rank shoulder boards and gold navy wings. LOC

CHAPTER 6
THE ENEMY BELOW

Military submarines were first pioneered during the American Revolution with the American *Turtle*, which attempted to sink the HMS *Eagle* in 1776. Various efforts were made with limited success over the following years until the American Civil War, when both sides created submersible craft. It was, however, the Confederate vessel *H.L. Hunley* that succeeded in sinking the USS *Housatonic* in 1864 with a spar torpedo, forever changing naval warfare. These early craft were man-powered and the torpedoes had to be attached to the target and detonated by the attacking sub.

Over the next half-century, naval designers created motorized submarines and perfected a torpedo powered by pressurized air. By 1900, John Holland had developed a dual-motor system that allowed submarines to run diesel engines on the surface and electric motors when submerged. These boats were adopted by the United States and Japan, among others. Both the Germans and the Russians were using submarines by 1903. The Russo-Japanese war of 1904–5 saw limited use of submarines but did have the first war patrol of seven Russian craft. This was not lost on the Germans.

August 1914 saw the first flotilla of ten U-boats (*Unterseeboot*) sail from Heligoland into the North Sea, where they sank three British warships. The German navy began the war with twenty-nine U-boats, which were used in the Atlantic, the North Sea, the Mediterranean, and during the Gallipoli campaign. The boats were armed with a new self-propelled torpedo, which

had a dual effect: a direct explosion and the added impact of a large steam bubble created by the initial explosion. The steam bubble lifted the ship, weakening the keel; when the steam subsided, the ship would drop in the center, breaking the keel in half.

U-boats usually operated on the surface, where they traveled faster and preyed mostly on merchant shipping. At first, they would stop the freighters, allow the crews to escape in lifeboats, and then sink the vessel and cargo with deck guns to conserve their torpedoes. When the British devised Q-ships, small trawlers or merchantmen with hidden guns, to lure U-boats close and sink them, it ironically led to the loss of more lives, as the U-boats began to attack while submerged, with no warning to the crews.

Initially, U-boats were used to enforce a blockade of the British Isles, sinking merchant ships and warships when possible. In 1916, the RMS *Lusitania* was sunk by the *U-20*, causing the United States to threaten to sever diplomatic ties. The German submarine fleet maintained its blockade until the indecisive action at Jutland, when it resumed its campaign on merchant ships.

In 1917, Germany announced a campaign of unrestricted submarine warfare and sank three American ships in March, bringing the United States into the war. Initially successful, this strategy led to the convoy system, which dramatically reduced the loss of tonnage to U-boats. By war's end, the U-boats had destroyed over 11 million tons of shipping. Of the 360 U-boats built during the war, 178 were lost.

Secretary of the Navy Josephus Daniels stands with his aide and son, Commander Daniels. Daniels is most remembered for his appointment of Franklin D. Roosevelt as assistant secretary of the navy, thrusting FDR into the national political arena. LOC

Assistant Secretary of the Navy Franklin D. Roosevelt (fifth from the left) attends the launch of the USS *Tennessee* on April 30, 1919. LOC

A German submarine in rough seas. Germany's reinstitution of unrestricted U-boat warfare proved intolerable to Americans, bringing the United States into the war. NARA

The engine room of an oil-burning German submarine. NARA

A riveter at work at Hog Island Shipyard, Philadelphia, Pennsylvania, in 1918. NARA

Women served as rivet heaters and passers-on in ship construction work, including at the shipyard in Puget Sound, Washington. NARA

Twenty-five Native Americans from the Carlisle Indian College in Pennsylvania learn to build ships at Hog Island, Philadelphia, Pennsylvania. NARA

Hellen Keller christens a United States Emergency Fleet ship launched in Los Angeles Harbor, California. The newly completed ship was the twelfth boat launched by the Los Angeles Shipbuilding and Dry Dock Company. NARA

A wooden ship built for United States Shipping Board Emergency Fleet Corporation by Pacific American Fisheries, Bellingham, Washington. NARA

Launching the *Quistconck*, the first ship completed at Hog Island shipyards. President Wilson and his wife are standing on the platform on opposite sides of the flagpole; Mrs. Wilson christened the vessel. NARA

This photo of Shop Number 2 at Bethlehem Steel Company in Pennsylvania, shows naval 6-inch guns with their mounts in the foreground; immediately in the rear are slides, or cradles, for 10-inch, 12-inch, and 14-inch guns. NARA

A last-minute escape from a vessel torpedoed by a German sub. The vessel's bow has already sunk into the waves, and the stern is slowly lifting out of the water. Men can be seen sliding down the ropes as the last lifeboat is pulling away. NARA

Rescued passengers from the French liner *Santay* climb up the sides of a French gunboat that came to the rescue. The *Santay* was torpedoed and sunk by a German submarine on April 10, 1918, while en route from Marseilles to Salonika. NARA

U.S. sailors in New York visit the captured U-boat *UC 5*, on display for a Liberty Bond drive. LOC

Another view of the *UC 5* on display in New York. LOC

In a most remarkable postwar incident, two German U-boats sunk during the war washed up on the rocks at Falmouth, England. The occurrence seemed to symbolize the end of the German navy. NARA

The battleship USS *Arkansas* was armed with a main battery of twelve 12-inch guns and capable of a top speed of 20.5 knots. Her speed and firepower served as a deterrent to U-boat attackers. Although she did not see significant action during the war, *Arkansas* was attached to the British Grand Fleet. NARA

The USS *Allen* convoys the USS *Leviathan*. *Allen* was a destroyer, the workhorse of the antisubmarine fleet, and escorted one of the first convoys of American servicemen across the Atlantic. After reaching Europe, it served in a joint task force that patrolled against U-boats and escorted convoys on their final leg of the Atlantic crossing. During escort duty, the *Allen* engaged a number of U-boats, but was credited with no kills. One of the vessel's final wartime duties was escorting the transport *George Washington*, which brought President Woodrow Wilson to the Versailles Treaty negotiations. NARA

The death of 128 Americans on the RMS *Lusitania* almost brought America to the brink of war; when tempers steadied, President Wilson declared that "America was too proud to fight." LOC

CHAPTER 7
VEHICLES OF WAR

World War I saw the first extensive combat use of motorized vehicles. Motor ambulances sped up evacuation of the wounded and saved lives, while American Liberty trucks became the first true mass-produced military motor transport. Designed by the Army Quartermaster Corps, almost 10,000 Liberty trucks were produced, with 7,500 serving overseas in the AEF. The Liberty's four-speed transmission and 52-hp engine allowed for a dizzying top speed of about 15 miles per hour. The truck became one of the logistical backbones of the AEF, ferrying supplies and soldiers across the front.

Perhaps the most significant motorized combat development of the war was the tank. Envisioned as a modern-day replacement for cavalry, the tank was intended to overcome the obstacles of modern war: trenches, barbed wire, machine guns, and artillery fire. The early years of the war saw the advent of armored cars—civilian motor cars with machine guns but scant armor—used in scouting roles. The British, reaching back to the designs of Leonardo da Vinci, began research in the Admiralty with the intent of creating a "landship." The British Mk I made its combat debut in 1915, shrouded in secrecy; it was referred to in communications as a "tank" in an attempt to list it as simply a water-storage vessel. The original design was based on the tracked chassis of the American Holt tractor. The low-slung nature of this arrangement led to the vehicle becoming stuck when crossing trenches, and the British subsequently went to a rhomboid shape with the tracks encircling the entire side of the tank.

As the British were perfecting the Mk I and its successors, the Mk II through Mk V, the French developed two tanks, the Schneider and the Saint-Chamond, both still using the Holt–type suspension. They first were used in an assault on the Chemin des Dames in 1917. The Germans slowly responded with their own tank, the A7V, a cumbersome behemoth with a crew of eighteen men. At the same time, the British had designed a light tank, the Mk A Whippet, and the French developed the Renault FT-17. The FT-17 became the standard tank of the American forces; small and nimble, with a two-man crew, it was a huge leap forward in technology as the first tank with a revolving turret. Previous designs by all forces had fixed guns, which required the entire tank to be aimed in order to fire.

Tanks were armed with either field guns or machine guns. When the U.S. Tank Corps adopted an insignia, it chose a triangle made of equal sections of yellow, red, and blue to signify the tank's ability to provide the shock of the cavalry, the firepower of the artillery, and the offensive spirit of the infantry.

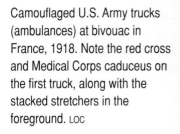

Camouflaged U.S. Army trucks (ambulances) at bivouac in France, 1918. Note the red cross and Medical Corps caduceus on the first truck, along with the stacked stretchers in the foreground. LOC

A Cadillac artillery tractor of Battery B, 140th Field Artillery Regiment, 39th Division, towing a field gun in training at Le Valdahon, France, in February 1919. NARA

The fire department at St. Nazaire, France was comprised of men drawn from Companies A, B, C, and D, 162nd Infantry Regiment, 41st Division, in January 1918. MHI

Three-ton Packard trucks of Water Service Train Number 2, attached to the 79th Division, take a break near Brabant-sur-Meuse, France, on November 3, 1918. NARA

Doughboys used some unique transportation. Here, 81st Division "Wildcats," the division's nickname, tame some French dogs in the summer of 1919. MHI

One of the Huns' locomotives taken by the boys of the 27th Division, under the command of Maj. Gen. John F. O'Ryan, at the town of St. Souplet, France, on October 9, 1918. NARA

This photo taken by Walter Zukowski, Company C, 107th Ammunition Train, 32nd Division, shows his unit learning to drive the new motorized tractors. MHI

This division poster on the side of a railway car leaves no doubt as to the future destination of the division, nor where it has been. MHI

Pvt. A. O. Donough from Company A, 7th Machine Gun Battalion, 3rd Division, drives an unidentified soldier in his sidecar in Germany, 1919. MHI

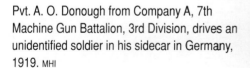

An unidentified member of the 319th Engineer Regiment, 8th Division, behind the wheel of a 1-ton locomotive in France, 1918. MHI

An unidentified 13th Division soldier relaxes on his truck's fender during a lull in training at Camp Lewis, Washington, in 1918. MHI

American Renault tanks of the 321st Company at the 302nd Tank Center at Varennes-en-Argonne, France, in October 1918. NARA

Thirteen-year-old Lee Gerard, a French boy who was adopted as a mascot of the 1st Tank Brigade. He was in action with the unit at St. Mihiel and the Argonne Forest and was gassed twice in action at Exermont. He was photographed with his tank at Varennes-en-Argonne, in October 1918. NARA

Sgt. Paul Postal of the 321st Tank Company and his mascot, "Mustard," which attached itself to the unit when it first went into action on Halloween 1918. NARA

Men of the 13th Engineer Regiment right derailed Engine 15 near Bugemont, France, February 1918. MHI

Pvt. Thomas Fargher (standing, center) of the 13th Engineer Regiment poses with some friends in front of Engine 34 in France in 1918. MHI

A mighty battalion of Mack war trucks, all for the Engineer Corps, manufactured by the International Motor Company in Allentown, Pennsylvania. NARA

Thirty 45-hp Holt Manufacturing Company "Caterpiller" tractors, comprising the motorized equipment of the 9th Field Artillery at Schofield Barracks, Hawaii. NARA

Front view of a two-man tank manufactured by Ford Motor Company in Detroit, Michigan. NARA

The army still used mules during the war. Here, Private Shook tries to move mules hauling an ammunition wagon stuck in the road and holding up the advance of the whole column at St. Baussant, east of St. Mihiel, France, on September 13, 1918. NARA

Traffic congestion on the roads behind the American lines in the Argonne was, at certain places, so great that the columns of vehicles were not able to move faster than 2 miles an hour. This scene, in the ruins of Esnes, France, in 1918, was typical. NARA

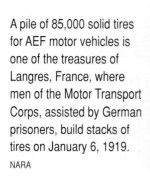

A pile of 85,000 solid tires for AEF motor vehicles is one of the treasures of Langres, France, where men of the Motor Transport Corps, assisted by German prisoners, build stacks of tires on January 6, 1919. NARA

Columns of German prisoners, taken by Americans in the first day of the assault on the St. Mihiel salient, march past a convoy of trucks and wagons on their way to the prison pens prepared for them at Ansauville, France, on September 25, 1918. NARA

This drawing by Capt. W. J. Duncan depicts French Army trucks and ambulances parked in the Place Carrière, Neufchâteau, France, headquarters of the Advance Section, Services of Supply. NARA

CHAPTER 8
PARIS—OOH LA LA!

At the eleventh hour on the eleventh day of November 1918, the Armistice was signed and peace was declared; people throughout the world celebrated in the streets with dancing, parades, champagne toasts, and cheering. Capt. Charles Normington of the 32nd Division described the scene in Paris in a letter to his parents:

. . . was on the street today when the Armistice with Germany was signed. Anyone who was not here can never be told or imagine the happiness of the people here. They cheered and cried and laughed and then started all over again. Immediately, a parade was started on the Rue des Italiennes and has been going on ever since. In the parade were hundreds of thousands of people from all over the world—soldiers from the U.S., England, Canada, France, Australia, Italy and the colonies. Each soldier had his arms full of French girls—some crying, others laughing. Each girl had to kiss every soldier before she would let him pass. The streets are still crowded and all traffic is held up.

There are some things such as this that never will be produced if the world lives a million years. They have taken movies of the crowd, but you can't get the sound or the expressions on the people's faces by watching the picture.

There is nowhere on earth I would rather be today than just where I am. Home would be nice and is next, but Paris and France are free after 4 years and three months of war.

And oh, such a war. The hearts of these French people have simply burst with joy. . . . Paris, that grand old city that has been dark for so long, is now all lighted up.

Many soldiers wrote of the overwhelming gratitude expressed by the French citizens. A few fortunate troops enjoyed accommodations in the finest hotels and were given the best foods and wines. Reaction to the wine and cognac were mixed, as they were a strange novelty for some and a savory pleasure for others. Some complained that every other store was a wine store, and that one taste had done them in. They concluded the only reason for its prolific availability was that the water must have been bad. Those who arrived with more refined palates raved about the wines and liquors served. Limited funds were an effective deterrent to enjoying the temptations that often characterized the city as a painted lady with her hand always out. However, the soldiers did agree that Paris was a wonderful city, the ladies were beautiful, and the food was delicious and plentiful.

African-American troops were welcomed by the French and respected for their fierce bravery, proven on the front lines as they fought at the side of the French Army. The 369th Harlem Infantry, known as the "Harlem Hellfighters," was honored with the Croix de Guerre for its valor by a grateful French government. Contradictory opinions of their color and culture were represented by France and America: The French welcomed them and celebrated their art and music, while they faced discrimination within the AEF. Their regimental band, under the direction of 1st Lt. James Reese Europe, raised morale by performing throughout France and changed the concept of music when they brought their unique style of jazz to Paris. The Parisians embraced this new sound and adopted it as their own.

As weeks passed, the lights and excitement of the city were displaced by longing for home and family. The endless wait for orders authorizing a return to the United States tried the patience of even the most resilient soldier. Several complained of being caught in a holding pattern of mind-numbing, repetitive duties. "Homesick as hell" was the refrain as the weeks passed into months.

One of the guns of Battery D, 105th Field Artillery, 27th Division, at Étraye, France, showing an American flag hoisted after the last shot had been fired when the Armistice took effect. NARA

Armistice celebration—Yanks and Tommies—in November, 1918. NARA

Luxembourg girls greet the American Army of Occupation. NARA

The Military Police Company of the District of Paris poses in the Jardin des Tuileries, Paris, April 1918. These troops are the 30th Company, 5th Regiment, United States Marine Corps. NARA

American and Allied soldiers enjoy themselves in the YMCA tea garden at 31 Avenue Montaigne, Paris. NARA

The headquarters building of the American forces in Germany occupied an entire block in Coblenz in1919. MHI

Military police on duty during the first snowstorm of the season, January 23, 1919, in Cochem, Germany. The sergeant, not on duty but enjoying the bracing air, is James Collers of the Motor Transport Corps. NARA

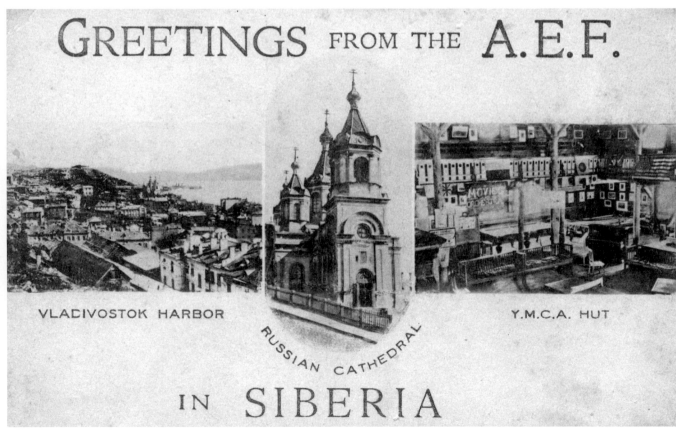

A postcard from the AEF in Siberia, 1918. Three AEF regiments were sent to Russia as the war ended. PRIVATE COLLECTION

Two military policemen pose with a Siberian and his Bactrian camel near Vladivostok, 1919. MHI

An unidentified American soldier poses with his Russian counterpart in front of a captured Red Army armored train near Lake Baikal, Russia, January 1920. MHI

Pvt. Teddy Raymond (left), trainer, and Pvt. Ritz Walters, middleweight boxer, in Paris in April 1919. Both men belonged to the 112th Field Artillery Regiment, 29th Division. NARA

Pvt. Milus F. Small, Jr. (in blackface), performs the opening number "Buttons" in the 29th Division show with some other "beauties" from the division at Bar-sur-Aube, France, in March 1919. NARA

Members of Company A, 112th Machine Gun Battalion, 29th Division, clown around with a mademoiselle. MHI

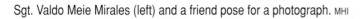

Sgt. Valdo Meie Mirales (left) and a friend pose for a photograph. MHI

The band of the 303rd Infantry Regiment, 76th Division, performs in front of the Palais des Fêtes de Paris, France, in November 1918.
NARA

Batteries A, B, C, and D of the 302nd Field Artillery Regiment, 76th Division, pass in review in 1918. NARA

Company I, 301st Infantry Regiment, 76th Division, pose at Versailles, France, June 1918. MHI

First Lt. John J. Maginnis poses with his "French Sweetheart" Jacqueline Punchon. Biguy, France, July 1918. MHI

Sgt. J. W. Killigrew of the 311th Ambulance Company, 78th Division, entertains some children in Authe, France, November 1918. NARA

A member of the 303rd Engineer Regiment, 78th Division, gets a haircut in France, 1918. MHI

Pvt. Jim Kay Wong of Cleveland, Ohio, on KP duty at 83rd Division Headquarters at Montigney-le-Roi, France, July 1918. NARA

Four soldiers of Company D, 310th Engineer Battalion, 85th Division, enjoy some R&R in Trier, Germany, on February 15, 1919. MHI

Soldiers of Company B, 310th Field Signal Battalion, 85th Division, stationed in Germany in 1919, practice with the heliograph. MHI

Lt. Frank S. Hugill attempts to retrieve his cap from a small admirer in France, 1918. MHI

Pvt. Walter T. O'Malley (circled) of Company B, 336th Machine Gun Battalion, 87th Division, poses with his company in France, January 1919. MHI

Officers of the 129th Field Artillery, 35th Division, at regimental headquarters at Château de Chanay near Courcemont, France, March 1919. Capt. Harry Truman is seated second row, third from right. NARA

This old castle perched on a hilltop above the Moselle River and the town of Cochem, Germany, was the headquarters of the U.S. Army IV Corps. In the foreground is Cpl. James C. Sulzer. January 9, 1919. NARA

A German fräulein is dressed in an army uniform in this cabinet card produced during the occupation. PRIVATE COLLECTION

The 369th "Harlem Hellfighters" Infantry Regiment band is generally credited with introducing jazz music to Europe. Here, 1st Lt. James Reese Europe conducts as members play at a concert. MHI

Lieutenant Europe and the 369th band play for patients of Hospital Number 9 in Paris on September 4, 1918. Sgt. Wood Andress, the first musician on the right, plays the slide trombone. NARA

The 369th concerts often closed with a performance by the "Percussion Twins," Herbert and Steve Wright. Herbert Wright brutally murdered James Reese Europe on the evening of May 9, 1919, following a perceived slight after a concert in Boston. MHI

A group of happy doughboys pose with some local French girls. PRIVATE COLLECTION

Roscoe S. Bowers sent this postcard from the station hospital at Coblenz, Germany, with the note, "Say Roger, what do you think of my hospital buddies [*sic*] 5-star Cognac?" PRIVATE COLLECTION

Four doughboys break into some French champagne; the fellow second from left appears to have had enough already. PRIVATE COLLECTION

Craps games were always a popular way to pass time, although gambling was generally frowned upon by AEF authorities. PRIVATE COLLECTION

Ambrose Sheler, of Shelby, Nebraska, sits for a portrait proudly showing off his 89th Division shoulder sleeve insignia and overseas stripe.
PRIVATE COLLECTION

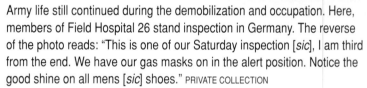

Army life still continued during the demobilization and occupation. Here, members of Field Hospital 26 stand inspection in Germany. The reverse of the photo reads: "This is one of our Saturday inspection [*sic*], I am third from the end. We have our gas masks on in the alert position. Notice the good shine on all mens [*sic*] shoes." PRIVATE COLLECTION

A soldier poses in Paris on May 25, 1919. Note the felt branch-colored flashes behind his collar disks; this unauthorized practice began and ended during the occupation period. PRIVATE COLLECTION

Three friends sport Army of Occupation shoulder sleeve insignia and wear branch-colored flashes denoting the Signal Corps (orange and white) behind their collar insignia in this occupation period photo. PRIVATE COLLECTION

This photo, dated October 1918 and simply inscribed, "To my Brother," shows the toll of combat on a young doughboy. PRIVATE COLLECTION

"A couple of chums," according to the inscription, these three infantrymen strike a studio pose in an alpine setting after the war. PRIVATE COLLECTION

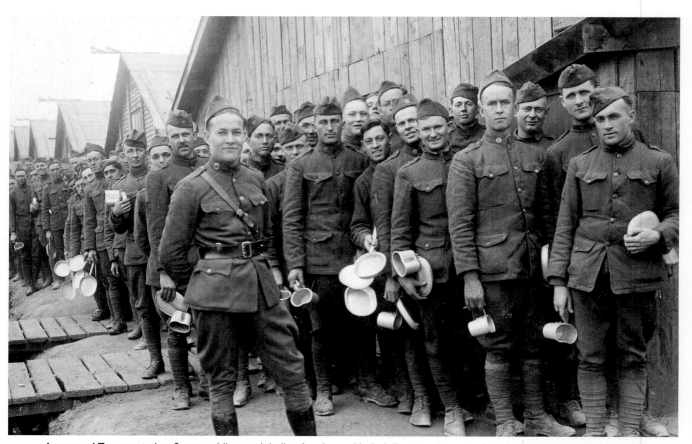

A group of Transportation Corps soldiers wait in line for chow with their lieutenant, somewhere in France. PRIVATE COLLECTION

Two members of the 2nd Engineers Regiment, 2nd Division, sit for the camera. Note the division shoulder sleeve insignia with the castle background denoting the engineer regiment. PRIVATE COLLECTION

A group of doughboys pose with French children in a recently liberated village. PRIVATE COLLECTION

Members of an engineer regiment repair roads destroyed by war. A note on the reverse of the photo states, "The fellow with the pipe in his mouth on this picture has our insignia on his left shoulder. How do you like it?" The soldier wears an Advance Section, Services of Supply, insignia. PRIVATE COLLECTION

Three friends stand for a portrait. The two men on the right wear Army of Occupation insignia. PRIVATE COLLECTION

Five officers at Beaune, France, in the spring of 1919. The officer on the right wears the triangular Tank Corps insignia. PRIVATE COLLECTION

V Corps soldiers feed a zebra somewhere in Europe. PRIVATE COLLECTION

A homesick medic writes to his brothers, saying, "How does this strike you fellows. [*sic*] Better come and give me a lift. Had this taken while on leave." PRIVATE COLLECTION

Three doughboys try out German pipes at Cochem. LOC

Soldiers had an opportunity to attend schools while serving overseas. Here, a group of doughboy scholars pose for a photo. PRIVATE COLLECTION

Cpl. Clifford C. Catlin, Company B, 31st Infantry Regiment, and friends pose in Russia in December 1918 as part of the Siberian Expedition. From left to right: Erickson, Chris Christensen, Adams, Renzo Crawford, and Catlin. PRIVATE COLLECTION

An unidentified member of the District of Paris, identified by his shoulder sleeve insignia, which features a fleur de lis, posed for this *carte postale*. PRIVATE COLLECTION

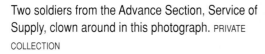

Two soldiers from the Advance Section, Service of Supply, clown around in this photograph. PRIVATE COLLECTION

A supply sergeant and friends make it to a more temperate part of France. PRIVATE COLLECTION

Col. William Wallace, commander of the 332nd Infantry Regiment, the one American regiment on the Italian front, shakes hands with General Guglielmotti, military attaché of the Italian war mission, aboard the *Duca D'Aosta* on the trip back to America. LOC

Chow time on the *Duca D'Aosta*; 332nd soldiers get a hot meal with other returning doughboys. The soldier on the far right wears a IV Corps insignia, the second soldier from the left a 6th Division insignia, and the soldier behind him a District of Paris shoulder sleeve insignia. LOC

Soldiers pass the time waiting for the Atlantic crossing home to finally end. PRIVATE COLLECTION

CHAPTER 9
HELLO MISS LIBERTY!

Two million soldiers returned from their service in France, Italy, and Russia between 1918 and 1923. They arrived as conquering heroes to parades and adulation—and to a fundamentally changed nation. Their experiences would set the stage for the Jazz Age and a second world war.

Homebound troops described the Statue of Liberty as the most beautiful thing in the world as they caught their first glimpse upon returning to the New York Harbor. Cheering crowds, honking tugboats, and bands welcomed them with familiar songs, and joyful tears were seen as the band struck up "Home Sweet Home." The Company D log of the 332nd Infantry Regiment described their thoughts: "This was their country, their people: here were their friends, their loved ones. This was the hour they had looked forward to for months: this judging from impressions of other countries, is best on earth, and this—this is 'Home Sweet Home' at last!"

Alfred Sutton, of the 308th Infantry Regiment, 77th Division, wrote in his diary, "The trip home on the S.S. *America* was so intensely satisfying that I made no journal entries whatever. I only want to mention here that there is no ecstasy that can equal the feeling that pulses through your being when you see that glorious lady with the torch welcoming you home."

Soldiers were transported by train to camps for processing and eventual discharge. Hundreds of parades were held throughout the country to honor them as they returned to their hometowns. The historian of one infantry regiment stated, "We at last separated, each man left for home deloused, discharged and delighted."

Many soldiers were assigned to the Army of Occupation and remained in Europe following the Armistice. Months after the war, their reception as they entered the home harbor was a stark contrast to the experiences of those who had returned earlier. As they docked, orders came down that Sam Browne belts were no longer allowed to be worn by officers. Military police were assigned to the docks to enforce this newly instituted War Department rule. Absent were the cheering crowds and honking tugboats. The nation had tired of war and was focused on the issues that arrived with the returning soldiers. Reemployment, displacements, pensions, and ongoing medical care requirements for the disabled challenged the government effort to streamline the federal budget. Another type of battle began for the doughboys as they formed lobbies and demonstrated in order to recover the entitlements that had been promised.

Some chose to bypass these struggles as they attempted to resume their former lives. Eric Lindquist of the 71st New York Infantry expressed his relief that the war was behind him:

> Leaving the terminal, I went out to Seventh Avenue, pinching myself in disbelief it was all over and we were free to go our way. An endless stream of people and traffic flowed by and as I stood observing, a sense of lightness came over me as with the thought foremost in my mind that I lived amongst free people and was proud of having paid my debt to society for the great privilege of citizenship. Without any hesitation, I joined the pulsating stream of life with a feeling society owed me nothing. The great right to strive and face the world with the peculiar and individual ability with which providence kindly endowed one was still retained. Horrid memories and old sores would without doubt continue to invade one's mind, but time has always provided a system of softening and healing the deepest of hurts.

As the years passed, the guns fell silent and the parades and memorials became a dim memory. Before long, the young soldiers and their contemporaries—who came of age in what seemed a distant time, when lives were sold cheaply and notions of idealism seemed quaint—were a forgotten generation of Americans. They bridged the Gilded Era and the Jazz Age; watched the fall of empires in bewildered awe; dreadfully witnessed the rise of Communism, Fascism, and Nazism; birthed the "Greatest Generation"; and opened an "American Century." They presided over the inauguration of a violent age they could never comprehend. Today, they beckon to us from the faded images in this book, extolling their love of family, home, and country. On the eve of this centennial, we must not overlook them. They shaped the modern world, underpinning it with all of its current virtue and depravity. Our world and our generation are yet their legacy.

The entrance to Camp Pontanezen, France, the primary debarkation marshaling area. This camp was the first stop on the way home for most doughboys. Note the insignia for the camp, as well as the representations of the 8th Division patches and the ubiquitous duckboard sidewalk that kept troops out of the mud. MHI

Old stone barracks used to house some of the troops at Camp Pontanezen. MHI

Some troops heading to the delousing station, the first stop on the trip home, at Camp Pontanezen, Brest, France. MHI

Camp Pontanezen headquarters, Brest, France. Note the duckboard construction of the arch bearing the camp insignia. MHI

Men of the 145th Field Artillery Regiment, 40th Division, board the SS *Santa Theresa* at Bordeaux, France, on December 23, 1918, for the return trip to America. NARA

The joy of waiting for chow before boarding the ship home is expressed in this comic postcard. PRIVATE COLLECTION

The YMCA Department for Reception of Returning Troops printed cards to both congratulate a job well done and announce the arrival of homecoming troops. PRIVATE COLLECTION

This card, part of a satirical set, depicts the moment a soldier sets foot on American soil. PRIVATE COLLECTION

A returning soldier, finally reunited with his sweetheart, finds his indispensable trench boots are not quite fitting for the parlor. PRIVATE COLLECTION

Home again—returning soldiers on the *Agamemnon* dock in Hoboken, New Jersey. NARA

THE UNIFORM IS LOVELY BUT OH YOU "KICKS"—

A returning doughboy greets his wife and baby at the Washington, D.C. station. LOC

Members of the famous "Harlem Hellfighters" 369th arrive in New York City. NARA

A welcome home
parade in honor of
returning members of
the AEF passes the
New York Public
Library. NARA

Colonel Donovan and the staff of the 165th Infantry, 42nd Division,
pass under the Victory Arch in New York City. NARA

Soldiers being mustered out at Camp Dix, New Jersey. NARA

Over 120,000 men did not return; some would rest in American cemeteries in France, England, and the Netherlands. This 1928 view of the American Battle Monuments Commission Aisne-Marne American Cemetery in France illuminates the true cost of war. NARA

One unknown soldier was selected to represent all of his comrades in arms. His body was returned to the United States for burial at Arlington National Cemetery, Virginia. Here, President Harding places a wreath of flowers on the casket of the Unknown Soldier in the rotunda of the Capitol on November 9, 1921. NARA

Most got on with their lives. In this wedding photo, the soldier wears three service stripes, indicating eighteen months service overseas, and a star designating early enlistment. PRIVATE COLLECTION

Archer J. Jewell, 14th Railway Engineers, returns home to his sweetheart. PRIVATE COLLECTION

After serving in three grueling campaigns during eighteen months in Europe, a returning member of the 1st Division poses with his girl. PRIVATE COLLECTION

A soldier arrives back on the farm!
PRIVATE COLLECTION

A father, wearing a Railhead Regulating Station shoulder sleeve insignia and three overseas service stripes, is at last reunited with his son. PRIVATE COLLECTION

Picking grapes was twice the fun for this returning 3rd Division soldier and his darling. PRIVATE COLLECTION

A group of pals from the 33rd Division pose for a photo at the National Photo Studio in New York shortly after arrival. PRIVATE COLLECTION

Home again! PRIVATE COLLECTION

This Haverstraw, New York, hand-tinted portrait immortalizes a young member of the Advanced Section, Service of Supply, just returned from France; the unknown soldier proudly wears his red discharge stripe and a chevron indicating six months overseas. MHI

An unidentified sergeant and his wife pose for a portrait upon his return from France. MHI

This magnificent color-tinted portrait of an unidentified Regular Army soldier in the 3rd Battalion, 25th Infantry Regiment, with two years of overseas service, as illustrated by his four six-month overseas service chevrons, was probably taken at Schofield Barracks, Hawaiian Territory. The medal is most likely a Mexican Border Service Medal; he also wears an expert rifleman badge. MHI

A portrait of an unidentified officer, possibly Capt. Arthur C. Newmann, from a Richmond, Virginia, estate; note the District of Columbia World War One service medal. MHI

Capt. Elijah Reynolds, 368th Infantry Regiment, 92nd Division, served as first sergeant of Company F, 25th Infantry Regiment, in the Regular Army for thirty years before finally obtaining a commission. MHI

ACKNOWLEDGMENTS

This work drew extensively from the manuscript and photographic collections of the National Archives of the United States (NARA), College Park, Maryland; the photo archives of the Library of Congress (LOC), Washington, D.C.; the manuscript and photo holdings of the U.S. Army Center of Military History (CMH), Washington, D.C.; the photographic collections of the Army Heritage and Education Center (MHI), Carlisle, Pennsylvania; the photographic collections of the U.S. Marine Corps History Division (MCHC), Quantico, Virginia; and the archives and photographic collections of the American Battle Monuments Commission (ABMC), Arlington, Virginia, and Garches, France. Each of these organizations continues to support our decades-long scholarship of World War I, and each has enriched this work. Their helpful staff members are ever ready to provide professional advice and assistance.

Our thanks go to Dr. Mitch Yockelson at the National Archives; Col. Bob Patrick, USA (Ret.), at the Library of Congress; Alan Bogan, Dr. Charlie Cureton, Sara Forgey, Bryan Hockensmith, John Pascal, Chris Semancik, Roxann Showers, and Dr. Richard Stewart at the U.S. Army Center of Military History; and Dave Bedford, Alec Bennett, Sen. Max Cleland (Ret.), Mike Conley, Mike Coonce, Dr. Alison Finkelstein, Geoffrey and Jennifer Fournier, William Gwaltney, Sarah Hermann, Michael Knapp, Tim Nosal, Michael Shipman, and John Wessels at the American Battle Monuments Commission.

Our particular thanks to Don Troiani for his generosity in sharing the remarkable photographic resource he created at the Military and Historical Image Bank; and to the collectors who graciously opened their homes and collections to us, including Art Beltrone, Dan Griffin, Scott Kraska, Dave and Steve Johnson, Ron Northrup, Hayes Otoupalik, Gus Radle, Bugsy Sigel, and Ryan Witte. Thanks to Dave Reisch and Brittany Stoner at Stackpole Books.

To the U.S. World War One Centennial Commissioners, Dr. Mary Cohen, Dr. Libby O'Connell, Edwin Fountain, John Hamilton, Jerry Hester, Tom Moe, Jim Nutter, Dr. Monique Seefried, Jim Whitfield, and Gen. Freddie Valenzuela, thanks for all you do to memorialize the deeds and legacy of the forgotten World War One generation.